Interpersonal Influence

LADD WHEELER

New York University

ALLYN AND BACON, INC.   BOSTON

To Little Mother, Tex, and Lynn

LIBRARY OF CONGRESS CATALOG CARD NUMBER: 73-108766

PRINTED IN THE UNITED STATES OF AMERICA

SECOND PRINTING . . . JANUARY, 1971

Contents

Acknowledgments

This book is a product of a graduate seminar I taught at Duke University in 1967-68. I owe deep appreciation to the students: Kent Butzine, Joel Cooper, Al George Goethals, Larry Gruder, Tom Hammock, Russell Jones, Jim Robinson, Kelley Shaver, Larry Ward, and Bob Wicklund.

Bibb Latané made many invaluable suggestions about the organization of the book, and Mary Wheeler forced me to be clear.

My beautiful, faithful, and hard-working secretary, Brigitte Sokolowsky, has been a dream, taking care of many chores so that I could write.

Preparation of this volume was facilitated by the resources of the Research Center of Human Relations, New York University, under the direction of Harold Basowitz.

I would like to express appreciation to the following publishers for permission to use quotations, tables, and figures from their publications:

American Psychological Association: Leon Festinger, "Informal social communication" in *Psychological Review, 57* (1950); Ladd Wheeler, "Toward a theory of behavioral contagion" in *Psychological Review, 73* (1966).

Appleton-Century-Crofts: Alan Kerckhoff and Kurt Back, *The June Bug: A Study of Hysterical Contagion* (published by the Educational Division, Meredith Corporation, 1968).

Clark University Press: C. C. Murchison, ed., *Handbook of Social Psychology* (1935).

Harper & Row Publishers, Inc.: Kurt Lewin, *Field Theory in Social Science*, ed. D. Cartwright (1951); Muzafer Sherif, *The Psychology of Social Norms* (published by Harper Torchbooks, 1936).

Holt, Rinehart and Winston, Inc.: E. E. Maccoby, T. M. Newcomb, and E. L. Hartley, eds., *Readings in Social Psychology*, 3rd ed., (1947); Theodore M. Newcomb, *Personality and Social Change* (1943); G. Mandler, et al., *New Directions in Psychology III* (1967).

Houghton Mifflin Company: F. H. Allport, *Social Psychology* (1924).

International Universities Press: K. R. Eissler, ed., *Searchlights on Delinquency* (1949).

Plenum Publishing Company: Festinger, Gerard, Hymovitch, Kelley, and Raven, "The influence process in the presence of extreme deviates" in *Human Relations, V* (1952); Hoffman, Festinger, and Lawrence, "Average points per trial earned by A. Average percent of terminal coalitions having A as a member" in *Journal of Human Relations, VII* (1954); Leon Festinger, "A theory of social comparison processes" in *Journal of Human Relations, II* (1954); Norman Polansky, Ronald Lippitt, and Fritz Redl, "An investigation of behavioral contagion in groups" in *Journal of Human Relations, 3* (1950); Ronald Lippitt, Norman Polansky, and Sidney Rosen, "The dynamics of power" in *Journal of Human Relations, 5* (1952).

Prentice-Hall, Inc.: Solomon E. Asch, *Social Psychology* (1952).

G. P. Putnam's Sons: W. McDougall, *Group Mind* (1920).

Stanford University Press: Stanley Schachter, *The Psychology of Affiliation* (1959).

University of Texas: H. T. Moore, "The comparative influence of majority and expert opinion," *American Journal of Psychology, 32* (1921).

Preface

Speaking very broadly, interpersonal influence has occurred whenever the actions of one or more individuals influence the actions, attitudes, or feelings of one or more other individuals. Such a definition is much *too* broad, however, because it encompasses almost everything in social psychology.

Social psychologists have, over the years, excluded a number of types of social or interpersonal influence from that category which they refer to as "interpersonal influence." Accordingly, this book will not deal with leadership, which is a category of research and theory unto itself. It will not deal with attitude organization and change. It will not deal with the socialization process. It will not deal with the relations between groups. It will not deal with bargaining. It will not deal with social perception. It might, however, touch upon any of these areas. In short, "interpersonal influence" is not a logical area which can be adequately defined.

Like many areas of thought, interpersonal influence has been historically defined. That is, a succession of men over the years have influenced one another, have agreed that the essence of these processes could be called interpersonal influence.

Consistent with a historical definition of "interpersonal influence," the major contributions to this area will be discussed in roughly chronological order. Too often the reader is exposed to a barrage of theories and experiments which he never really understands. Not knowing the course of development of an area, it is difficult to understand why psychologists are currently concerned with the things they are concerned with. Only major positions will be included in this historical approach, and few experiments will be described. As much as possible, the focus will be on theory.

Hopefully, but as is rarely the case, the reader will devote more time to thought than to memorization. Hopefully, he will see beyond the final page.

My greatest delight would be to hear a fine social psychologist say, a few years from now, that he was initially attracted to the area because of this book. But I will be satisfied if the reader gains a better understanding of and keener interest in the social influence processes surrounding him.

LADD WHEELER

New York City
April 1970

The Early Years: 1900-1935

Norman Triplett was a research psychologist at the Indiana University Psychological Laboratory in the latter part of the nineteenth century. He was also a bicycle-racing enthusiast and authority. As a result of these two facts he conducted, in 1895, the first experiment in social psychology.

Because of his enthusiasm for bicycle racing (and perhaps in order to place a winning bet), Triplett often studied the records of the Racing Board of the League of American Wheelmen.

He noticed that when riders raced against one another in direct competition, the times were much faster than when a single rider raced against the clock. A third type of race, in which a single rider raced against the clock but was paced by some other vehicle, produced an intermediate speed.

In order to account for these facts, Triplett proposed the *theory of dynamogenesis*. This theory stated that "the bodily presence of another rider is a stimulus to a racer in arousing the competitive instinct; that another can thus be the means of releasing or freeing nervous energy for him that he cannot of himself release; and, further, that the sight of movement in that other is perhaps suggesting a higher rate of speed, is also an inspiration to greater effort" (Triplett, 1897, p. 516).

Triplett reasoned that if this theory were true, it would hold for activities other than bicycle racing. In order to test the theory, he gave children the task of winding fishing reels—both alone or in direct competition. Twenty of the 40 subjects wound the reels faster in competition, while only 10 of the subjects wound faster when alone. Triplett concluded that the experiment had supported the theory.

It should be noted that the theory of dynamogenesis contains two separate factors. First, the arousal of the competitive instinct releases latent energy. Second, the sight of movement in others suggests a higher rate of speed. This latter factor is a special case of another theory—the *ideo-motor theory*.

According to the ideo-motor theory, actions tend to be associated with the idea of the action. And through the constant paring of thought with its subsequent expression in behavior, the very idea of a response comes to lead to the response itself. An idea, in other words, leads to a motor response corresponding to the idea. In the case of the theory of dynamogenesis, the idea of movement is produced by observation of someone moving, and the idea leads to faster movement.

After Triplett's experiment, psychologists became concerned with analytically separating the various factors which could produce faster performance in groups. Among other things, the effect could be due to (1) mere observation of someone else performing the same task, (2) a feeling of competition, or (3) *being* observed by others.

Floyd H. Allport performed a number of experiments in which performance of individuals working alone was compared with the performance of individuals working in groups. In order to eliminate competition as a factor, Allport specifically instructed subjects not to compete. In fact, subjects were forbidden to compare results. On numerous tasks, such as free chain association, vowel cancellation, reversible perspective, and multiplication, subjects worked faster when in groups than when alone. Allport coined the term "social facilitation" to describe the faster group performance.

Social facilitation was said to be due to the sight and sound of others doing the same thing. Allport explained this as follows:

Since we usually both hear and see ourselves work we might suppose that the sound and sight of our movements become conditioning stimuli; and that they tend to re-evoke or augment in us these very movements from which they were derived. Similar movements made by others, since they give similar stimulations, would then serve the same purpose (Allport, 1924, pp. 283-284).

Although Allport believed this explanation of social facilitation in terms of conditioning to be true generally, he realized that "attitudes of a more complex sort are also probable: knowing that those about us are to be doing the same task, we are disposed to work more rapidly *from the start*" (p. 284).

Rivalry, Allport believed, can never be entirely eliminated; it also contributes to faster performance in groups. "The visceral reaction in rivalry, as in other emotions, probably liberates internal secretions, and involves other responses characteristic of the sympathetic system. By this means a higher level of energy is provided for the competitive exertion" (p. 283).

Allport did not find that all of the effects of working in a group were favorable. On a test requiring subjects to refute philosophical arguments, performance was qualitatively poorer in a group than alone. Allport believed this to be due to distraction and over-excitement, and that the positive effects of working in a group usually overweighed the negative effects; thus the choice of the term "social facilitation."

Allport had attempted to eliminate competition from his experiments but was aware that some degree of rivalry was undoubtedly present. In a further attempt to assess the role of competition, experiments were conducted in which subjects were told to compete. For example, Whittemore had subjects print out copies of newspaper material with rubber stamps, being told to assume either a competitive or a non-competitive stance. He found that all twelve subjects did more work in the competitive situation, but that it was of inferior quality (Whittemore, 1924).

Whittemore believed that the mere non-competitive observation of others doing the same thing leads to faster performance (as argued by Allport) and that competition produces emotional reinforcement which summates with the external social cues. The poorer quality of performance can again be explained by distraction and over-excitement.

In all of the experiments described so far, subjects working in groups were of course in position to be observed by the other group members. Perhaps the desire to make a good impression, or equivalently, the apprehension about not making a good impression, caused subjects to work harder and faster. In order to test this possibility, Dashiel (1935), a student of Allport, conducted a series of experiments in which subjects worked on multiplication problems, analogies, and a serial association test (in which the subject produced a chain of associated words).

In an *Audience* condition, one subject worked at a small table while two other students seated at the table observed him very closely. The subject was thus apprehensive about his performance being evaluated by the audience. Undoubtedly, this condition also included strong competition, because the three students took turns as problem-solvers and observers.

In a *Competition* condition, subjects worked together in groups of 15 with instructions to compete with one another. A third condition, the *Together* condition, required subjects to work together in groups of 15 with instructions not to compete.

In the *Alone-Simultaneous* condition, a number of subjects worked in separate rooms during periods of time signalled to them by a buzzer. In a final condition, the *Alone* condition, a subject worked alone in a room at a time when no other subjects were working.

The combination of competing and of being closely observed, a combination produced in the *Audience* condition, produced the fastest performance of all. The *Alone* condition, on the other hand, produced the slowest performance.

The *Together* condition, the *Alone-Simultaneous* condition, and the *Competition* condition produced approximately the same results, although the *Competition* subjects were somewhat faster. It is possible that stronger instructions to compete in the *Competition* condition could have produced greater differences, but what is interesting and important is the equivalent performance in the *Together* and *Alone-Simultaneous* conditions. It suggests that the *physical* presence of others is not important; rather, feeling *psychologically* part of a working group enhances performance. This in turn is probably due to a somewhat inescapable feeling of competition.

In general, the quality of performance was higher in the slower groups, and one may question use of the term "social facilitation." Because the term is a historical fact, accept it, but bear in mind that energy output is the only thing facilitated.

Because energy output is important only for relatively simple tasks, experiments requiring complex thought or reasoning failed to produce social facilitation effects. In fact, the opposite effect, "social inhibition" was often obtained. The explanation offered was that other people were distracting stimuli when group members were trying to think.

Very few questions about social facilitation were answered decisively in these years. New interest in the problem has recently appeared, and we will return to the topic in later chapters.

Some characteristics of the early years

One characteristic of this period is that researchers were interested primarily in the product of groups and not in the process by which the product emerged. Along with this, subjects were not asked for their subjective evaluations of the group experience. The reader should watch for the gradual shift in emphasis from *what* the group produced to *how* the group produces, and from what is done experimentally to the individual to what the individual reports as his reaction to what was done.

There was also more interest in application than in understanding. One reason for the interest in social facilitation is that it had implications for education and for industry. As the field matured in later years, understanding for the sake of understanding became the central motivation.

There was little, if any, theory about interpersonal influence. This may be due to the feeling that no new theorizing was needed—that an adequate account of social behavior required no theoretical concepts other than those dealing with individual behavior. Dashiell wrote that "it is to be borne in mind that in the subjective stimulus-response relationship of an individual to his fellows we have to deal with no radically new concepts, no principles essentially additional to those applying to non-social situations" (Dashiell, 1935, p. 1097). Such a statement could be taken to mean that no new and supra-individual qualities arise when a group is formed; thus, there need be no special theories about social behavior.

In fact, if there was an underlying theoretical question of this period, it was whether there was behavior distinctly social in nature and requiring a "social" psychology.

The "Group Mind" controversy

The major controversy of this era was whether or not a group has any properties which do not reside in the individual members of the group. The major protagonists were William McDougall and F. H. Allport.

McDougall's The Group Mind (1920) defined a mind as "an organized system of mental or psychical forces." Any highly organized human society, argued McDougall, is a system of mental or purposive forces and may thus be said to have a collective mind. The group mind is a property of the group rather than the individuals in the group because the individuals of a society can be gradually replaced by other individuals without necessarily changing the system of forces operating in the society.

According to McDougall, there are five criteria for the existence of a group mind: (1) Continuity of existence, with the individual replaceable. (2) In the minds of members there must be an idea of the group. (3) Interaction with other groups, especially rivalry and conflict, promotes a group self-sentiment. (4) Existence of a body of traditions and customs in minds of members. (5) Specialization of functions and division of labor.

Although this sounds reasonable, McDougall sounded almost frightened to espouse the doctrine. "I know well that very many readers may at first find themselves repelled by this notion of a group mind and that some of them will incline to regard it as a fantastic fad of an academic crank" (McDougall, 1920, p. 26).

As a matter of fact, many readers did. Foremost among them was Allport. He argued that whatever is there is only in the minds of the individuals and that if all the individuals perished at one time, "the so-called 'group mind' would be abolished forever" (Allport, 1924, p. 9). All psychology, even social psychology, is a psychology of the individual, because only the individual possesses consciousness. Other people are merely stimuli which impinge upon the consciousness of the individual.

McDougall and Allport agreed that the group or society into which an individual is born influences the ideas, thoughts, and habits of that person. They agreed that one could gradually replace the members of a society and maintain the essence of the original society. They agreed that the group as such does not possess a collective consciousness; only individuals possess consciousness.

Where did they disagree? Merely in that McDougall wished to use the term "group mind" and Allport did not. The latter believed that such terms would divert attention from "the locus of cause and effect, namely, the behavior mechanism of the individual" (Allport, 1924, p. 9).

Allport believed that the proper study of psychology was the motivation of the *individual,* how the *individual* learns, how the *individual* perceives, and how the *individual* organizes his attitudes and sentiments. To study the "group mind" of a nation is to ignore everything that is scientifically important and to consider only gross changes and broad trends.

The many psychologists, in addition to Allport, who attacked the "group mind" concept had additional reasons for doing so. The concept was suspiciously similar to sociological and philosophical concepts tinged with mysticism. In particular, it was similar to Hegel's idealistic philosophy—which included the belief that there is only one divine and absolute Mind which reveals itself in history and particularly in the historical development of nations. In 1920 German nationalism was of course not very popular, and McDougall even went to some effort in the introduction to *The Group Mind* to damn Germany. He himself realized that one objection to this concept would be its superficial similarity to Hegelian Mind.

The controversy was never resolved, although McDougall did eventually admit to a "tactical error" in using the term "group mind." In later chapters we will see that the bramblebush of polemic at least produced empirical berries.

2

Muzafer Sherif:
The Psychology of Social Norms
1936

Sherif published this important book at the age of 30, one year after he had received his Ph.D. Having been reared in Turkey, he was very much aware of cultural differences and had studied cultural anthropology and sociology. On two grounds he disagreed with those who had espoused a social psychology of the individual, particularly with F. H. Allport.

The first disagreement concerned Allport's explanation of the greater energy released in a group situation. He had attributed social facilitation to the sight and sound of others doing the same thing. Sherif argued that individuals raised in a noncompetitive society might react quite differently to the sights and sounds of others doing the same thing.

For individuals raised in the highly competitive American society, the sight of someone else doing the same thing is a conditioned stimulus for speeding up—lest one lose the race and die poor and unknown. In a different culture, however, the sight of someone else doing the same thing might be a stimulus for ceasing the activity altogether—competition being unmanly and ungodly. Sherif believed that Allport had stopped at a level of explanation where psychology should actually begin.

Sherif's second disagreement with Allport concerned the latter's position in his debate with McDougall on the group mind question. Allport had argued that a group is merely a collection of individuals and that no new and supra-individual qualities arise when individuals come together and form a group. Sherif agreed that "if you throw all the individuals of a nation into the ocean there will be no nation" (Sherif, 1963, p. 83), but he also said that "the pattern of the social situation creates a psychological atmosphere that is not inherent in its discrete parts" (p. XV).

Sherif believed that when people interact, norms develop. Norms are expected modes of behavior and belief established by a group. They facilitate interaction by specifying what is expected and acceptable behavior in a particular situation. Following the sociologist Durkheim, Sherif believed norms to have the properties of exteriority and constraint. They are to some extent outside of or exterior to any one individual, and they constrain the individual to behave in certain ways.

Sherif's argument may be stated as follows: New norms arise when people interact in fluid and ambiguous situations which contain a number of behavioral alternatives. Further, the norms persist and guide the behavior of individuals even when the individuals are no longer a part of the group in which the norm was formed.

Sherif believed he could win his point by experimentally demonstrating the formation of group norms which would then influence individual behavior outside of the group. In order to do this, he needed a situation sufficiently ambiguous that individuals could influence one another toward a common norm.

The autokinetic effect appeared to be a useful phenomenon. It is produced when one views a pinpoint of light in a completely dark room. The light cannot be localized definitely because there is nothing in reference to which you can locate it. Thus the light appears to move even if one knows perfectly well that it is not moving. It appears to move in different directions and for different distances.

In one set of conditions, the subjects were first tested alone. The subject sat at a small table on which there was a telegraph key. The following instructions were given:

> When the room is completely dark I shall give you a signal "ready" and then show you a point of light. After a short time

the light will start to move. As soon as you see it move, press the key. A few seconds later the light will disappear. Then tell me the distance it moved. Try to make your estimates as accurate as possible (Sherif, 1963, p. 95).

In all cases the light was left on for two seconds after the subject indicated the beginning of movement. Judgments were expressed in inches and fractions of inches, and one hundred judgments were obtained from each subject.

Under these conditions, subjects gradually established a stable range of estimated movement. The first three judgments might be 1 inch, 3 inches and 12 inches, showing great variability. But over time, variability decreased and subjects gave judgments lying between, say, 13 and 15 inches. The ranges that were established varied. A second subject might establish a range of, say, 2 inches to 5 inches. In other words, the subjects eventually established some order in a completely chaotic situation. Written introspective reports obtained from subjects after the experiment indicated that subjects compared each movement of the light with the previous movement.

Subjects who had established their own personal range of movement were then placed together in groups of two or three. Subjects were left free as to the order in which they would give their judgments, being told to give their judgment in random order as they pleased.

The results were clear-cut. Subjects tended to converge to a common norm of movement. When tested individually, groups-to-be had an average range of estimated movement of 3.6 inches. After three sessions as groups, the average range was .4 inches. This movement toward a common norm was gradual and mutual. It did not occur because one person remained rigid and the other subjects moved toward his judgments. Rather, all subjects tended to gradually change their estimate to be more similar to those of the other subjects.

In another set of conditions subjects experienced the autokinetic effect for the first time in groups of two and three. They had not established their own individual norms. Under these conditions the convergence toward a common norm was even faster and more complete than in the conditions just described. By the third session as a group, subjects had reduced the average estimated range of movement to less than .1 inches. These subjects were then tested alone to determine if the established group norm would influence individual judgments. Again the results were in the predicted direction. The average range of estimated movement was .6 inches, indicating some, but very little, movement away from the previously established group norm.

Sherif carried this research further by pairing a naive subject and an experimental confederate, or what we frequently in social psychology call a "stooge." The confederate had been instructed to make all of his judgments within a predetermined range. The aim of the experiment was to find out how much the judgments of the confederate would influence the judgments of the naive subject.

Again the results are clear-cut. The naive subject quickly adopted the range of judgments used by the confederate.

On the day following this session between the naive subject and the experimental confederate the subject was placed in the autokinetic situation alone. Would the subject continue to make his judgments within the range he had adopted working with the confederate? Or would he, now free of the confederate's influence, establish his own range of movement?

The results were quite consistent with those from the other experimental conditions. Subjects did indeed, within a very close degree, maintain the range of movement which the confederate had caused them to adopt in the first place.

From these several experimental conditions involving the autokinetic effect, Sherif wished to derive a very general conclusion about society, applicable to any group in any part of the world at any time in history.

> In short, when a group of individuals faces a new, unstable situation and has no previously established interest or opinions regarding the situation, the result is not chaos; a common norm arises and the situation is structured in relation to the common norm. Once the common norm is established, later the separate individuals keep on perceiving it in terms of the frame of reference which was once the norm of the group (Sherif, 1963, p. 111).

Sherif has shown us that individuals in groups do indeed form norms and that these norms are binding upon the individuals even in the absence of the group. We are left with two important questions. First, why are norms formed? And second, once a norm is formed, how does it get unformed or changed?

Sherif said that norms are formed in order to reduce uncertainty and confusion. Suppose that a small isolated tribe has experienced several years of drought, with consequent crop failure and starvation. Suddenly a rainstorm begins and in the midst of it a young virgin is struck by lightning. What is the meaning of this? Members of the tribe must come to a common understanding of the event. They may decide that the rain god wants the yearly sacrifice of a virgin. Or they may decide to build a temple at the spot and worship the girl. Or they may decide that this particular girl was the evil influence causing the drought, never allowing her name to be used again in the tribe. Whatever they decide will reduce the confusion in the situation and may lead to a lasting belief and mode of behavior which will be adopted by subsequent generations.

The second question mentioned above was "how do norms get changed?" Sherif argued that situations change, so that a norm that was useful or at least harmless at one point in time creates hardship and friction at another point in time. The people for whom the norm creates the greatest hardship revolt against it, refusing to continue to behave in a way that is clearly harmful to themselves. If the norm produces clear benefits for some members of society and hardships for others, there may be strife and bloodshed. The results may be complete destruction of the norm and the consequent change of society, or it may be destruction of those who revolt and the strengthening of the norm.

Norms develop because they are needed—to increase clarity, to promote interaction, to free individuals from having to make a decision about every aspect of behavior. They last until they produce unclarity, interfere with interaction, or create burdens for the majority of the group or society. They are maintained through social sanctions, punishment for those who disregard them and reward for those who obey them.

Entering a new group and adopting its norms is sometimes a tough procedure, because these norms may be in conflict with what one has known in the past. For a group to dissolve a norm may be extremely difficult. A few people may be pinched by the norm, but the majority of citizens accept it as a normal facet of living. The few may have to resort to extreme measures to overcome the inertia of the many.

3

Kurt Lewin: The Psychology of Social Climates

Kurt Lewin was one of the giants of psychology, making major contributions to Developmental, Personality, Learning, Perception, and Social Psychology. Many of the major social psychologists of today are either Lewin's students, or students of his students. The theoretical posture Lewin developed is the theoretical posture of modern social psychology. Despite the temptation to examine the whole body of Lewin's work, the subject matter of this book is interpersonal influence, and I will confine myself to Lewin's contributions to this area.

Although Lewin published as early as 1917, the first paper which we consider properly in the realm of interpersonal influence was published in 1939 with Ronald Lippitt and Ralph K. White (Lewin, Lippitt, and White, 1939). An expanded version of this research constituted Lippitt's doctoral dissertation, and the contributions of both Lippitt and White should not be minimized.

Lewin was Jewish and had left Germany partially because of persecution. In 1939 Hitler was continuing to expand his *Lebensraum,* and Lewin was quite naturally concerned about various types of government, with their corresponding social climates, and their effects upon the governed. He decided to investigate this by creating clubs of eleven-year-old boys and exposing each club to different leadership styles. The three leadership styles he chose to investigate were democratic, authoritarian, and laissez-faire. Each style of leadership is described below.

Authoritarian leadership: All decisions about club activities were made by the leader. Each decision was communicated to the group at the time it was to be implemented, never ahead of time. The leader remained at all times aloof from the group and gave praise or criticism without giving his reasons.

Democratic leadership: All decisions were made by group discussion with the leader taking an active and encouraging role. The leader encouraged the group to make long-range group goals. When asked for advice, the leader proposed alternatives for the group to discuss. The leader was always friendly and always gave factual reasons for his praise and blame.

Laissez-faire leadership: The leader was friendly although very passive, offering no suggestions or evaluations. He sat quietly, gave information if asked, and furnished work and play materials.

Each club met once a week for a number of weeks and the leadership style was changed from time to time, so that each club experienced each type of leadership. In addition to observing each meeting according to a controlled observation schedule, the experimenters devised several critical test situations: (1) the leader arrived late; (2) the leader was called out during the meeting; (3) the leader was called out, and a stranger entered the room and attacked the work of a group member and then the group as a whole.

Lewin expected the *Democratic* clubs to be more productive, more cohesive, and better able to carry on task activities in the absence of the leader. The *Laissez-faire* groups were expected to be somewhat frustrated by the lack of guidance and to spend a great deal of time in disorganized horseplay. The *Authoritarian* groups were expected to be severely frustrated by the repressive control exerted over them. How they would react to this frustration, however, was a question of great interest to Lewin and his colleagues.

On the one hand, frustration might lead to aggression toward one another, other clubs, and the leader. On the other hand, the authoritarian suppression would work against the expression of aggression. Depending upon the personalities of the group members and of the leader, the greater frustration of *Authoritarian* leadership might or might not be great enough to overcome the leader's suppressive control.

At this point we must consider the theoretical framework which generated this research.

Lewin conceived of action as occurring at certain levels, the level being determined by two sets of opposing forces (driving and restraining), which, taken together, constitute a force field. He applied this conceptual framework to the level of inter-member aggressiveness shown under the various leadership styles.

It is the nature of young boys to exhibit a certain amount of aggressiveness in their play and work activities; it is fun and it is a way to test one's wings. At the same time, there are opposing or restraining forces such as the friendship felt for the other boys, the concern that the leader might not approve of aggressiveness, and the formality of weekly club meetings. Driving forces (toward aggression) are at some point balanced exactly with the restraining forces. At this point we say that the resultant force is zero, meaning that the driving forces equal the restraining forces. This is known as a quasi-stationary equilibrium. It is called an equilibrium because the driving and restraining forces are equal, and it is called quasi-stationary because either driving or opposing forces may be added to the situation or taken away from the situation, thereby creating a new level of aggressiveness.

Figure 1a gives an example of the quasi-stationary equilibrium for aggressive acts which might be expected to exist in *Democratic* and *Authoritarian* groups. Although the subjects in *Authoritarian* groups are more frustrated, as shown by the heavier and more numerous arrows or forces pointing toward greater aggression, they exhibit less aggression than *Democratic* groups because the leader inhibits aggression, as shown by the stronger forces against aggression.

But what happens when the leader leaves the room? The forces pushing toward aggression remain strong, but most of the restraining forces disappear when the leader disappears, as shown in Figure 1b. The result is a dramatic increase in aggressive acts for *Authoritarian* groups; in contrast, not much change when the *Democratic* leader leaves the room; he has not been exerting strong restraining forces.

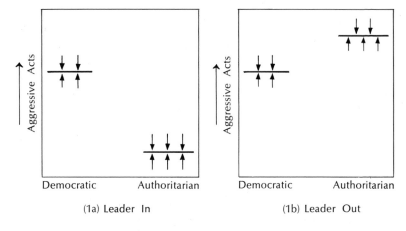

FIGURE 1.   Aggressive acts as a function of leadership type and
(1a) leader in the room, (1b) leader out of the room
(Lewin, 1947).

Figure 1 merely provides an illustration of the kind of theoretical position that provided the design of the experiment, but
the data actually obtained were in close accord with the theory.
The major findings were as follows:

1. The three leadership styles produced four resultant social
   atmospheres—*Democratic, Laissez-faire, Aggressive Autocracy,*
   and *Apathetic Autocracy.* Three of the four clubs reacted to
   Authoritarian leadership with apathy, dependence, and little
   capacity for initiating group action *(Apathetic Autocracy).*
   The remaining club under *Authoritarian* leadership demonstrated considerable frustration and some degree of aggression toward the leader *(Aggressive Autocracy).*

2. Whether the leader was in the room or not, the *Democratic*
   clubs spent the same amount of time in constructive activity.
   The *Authoritarian* groups, on the other hand, did far less
   work when the leader was out of the room.

3. When a previously *Apathetic Autocrat* group was changed to
   either *Democratic* or *Laissez-faire* leadership, there was a
   massive amount of horseplay on the day of transition. Horseplay having been prevented for six days by the *Authoritarian*
   leader, there was a need to "blow off" in the more permissive
   leadership situation.

4. When a stranger came in while the leader was out and insulted the group members, the *Democratic* clubs aggressed against the stranger, and when the stranger left, against inanimate objects. In contrast, the *Authoritarian* groups aggressed toward an out-group (another club meeting at the same time). Fearing the leader, they also feared other adults who entered the meeting area, and they reduced their aggressive needs by scapegoating against out-clubs.

5. Within *Authoritarian* groups, individual differences in behavior were far less than within the *Democratic* groups. This result was predicted from the quasi-stationary equilibrium model. With very strong forces driving toward aggression and very strong forces restraining aggression, members of the *Authoritarian* group found themselves in a vise of forces preventing the appearance of individual differences.

We have discussed the theoretical basis for this pioneer experiment and have summarized the major results. In later chapters we will return to the theoretical implications of the quasi-stationary equilibrium. The remaining point to be made here is that the experiment started a whole new type of methodology in social psychology.

This was the first attempt to create in the laboratory a specified social climate. The subjects were allowed to interact in a real life face-to-face situation. Observations were not confined to some final product of the group, but rather, group process was constantly monitored. While not methodologically pure, the experiment contained sophisticated controls. For example, the groups were composed initially of matched individuals, and there was an independent validation of the manipulated leadership styles. There were multiple dependent measures, such as careful observation interviews and sociometric measures. Perhaps most important of all, the experiment indicated to everyone that the complexity of social life could be studied in the laboratory with a high degree of precision.

The experiment included what we have come to call an "independent check on the manipulation" or a "validation of the manipulation." The various acts of the leaders were observed and coded into nine different categories in order to determine if the manipulated independent variable of the study, leadership, had been effectively created. The results were that the *Authoritarian*

leader was highest on giving orders, giving disrupting commands, making nonconstructive criticism, and giving praise and
approval. The *Democratic* leader, on the other hand, was highest
on giving guiding suggestions, on stimulating self-guidance, on
making matter-of-fact statements, and on being jovial and confident. The *Laissez-faire* leader was highest only on extending
information.

These results indicate that different leadership styles were
successfully created and in what ways they differed.

Several different types of data were collected:

1. A quantitative running account of the social interactions of the
    five children and the leader.
2. A minute-by-minute group structure analysis giving a record
    of activity subgroupings, whether the goals were initiated by
    the leader or the children, and the degree of unity.
3. An interpretive running account of significant actions and
    changes in the atmosphere of the group as a whole.
4. Continuous stenographic records of all conversations.

The children were also interviewed during each transition
period from one kind of leader to another in order to determine
how they felt about each one, how similar he was to parents,
and how similar he was to teachers. Parents themselves were
interviewed on the kind of discipline used in the home. Teachers
were asked about any changes in school and behavior as a function of club membership.

Members of each club were carefully matched on such
characteristics as intelligence, obedience, leadership, amount of
physical energy, and so forth. Furthermore, the use of sociometric
questionnaires administered in the classrooms from which the
club members were drawn made it possible to select groups
which were closely matched in terms of patterns of rejection,
friendship, and cohesiveness. All clubs met in a common setting
with identical material and equipment. In order to insure, at least
in the *Democratic* and *Authoritarian* groups, that the same patterns of activities would be engaged in, the clubs under the
Democratic leadership met first in time during the week; then the
activities which were selected by those clubs were automatically
assigned to the parallel clubs under the *Authoritarian* leadership. This is methodological sophistication.

Perhaps the best way to explain the importance of this experiment is to quote a summary of the authors themselves. One can not always trust an investigator to state the importance (or lack of it) of his own research objectively, but in this case one can. "It was found in this exploratory study that the process of small-group life could be experimentally manipulated in a satisfactory way for scientific study and could be recorded adequately for meaningful quantitative analysis" (Lewin, Lippitt, and White, 1939, p. 299). One might add that the theoretical development occasioned by the study was of extreme importance. We will encounter it again in later chapters.

4

The Effect of Majority Opinion:
H. T. Moore and Solomon Asch

In examining the research on interpersonal influence in the early years of experimental social psychology, one finds some work that is distinctly different from the social facilitation research described in Chapter 1. One very important such experiment on social influence was done by H. T. Moore in 1921.

Moore was concerned with the relative influence of majority and expert opinion upon the individual. Each subject was given three sets of paired comparisons: (1) Linguistic—choose the more offensive statement from each of 18 pairs, (2) Ethical—choose the more offensive character trait from each of 18 pairs, and (3) Musical—choose the preferred resolution of each of 18 pairs of musical chords.

Two days later each subject was again given these scales to establish a baseline number of reversals (the number of reversals one could expect in the absence of any influence). Some days after this, subjects were given the judgments of the majority of other students on each of the paired comparisons and were asked to rejudge the pairs. Two days after this, subjects were given the judgments of prestigious experts from the various fields and were asked to rejudge the pairs.

The number of judgment reversals in each condition is shown in Table 1. It is clear that both majority opinion and expert opinion influenced the subjects in their judgments. The amount of influence was about the same, except that the majority opinion was somewhat more influential on linguistic judgments.

Why should simply knowing the judgments of other people change one's own judgment? Moore believed that conformity is so frequently reinforced that the opinion of other people is a stimulus which elicits a conforming response. This is a reasonable explanation, because it is certainly true that conformity is rewarded or reinforced, while deviation is punished.

Solomon Asch did not, however, find the explanation reasonable, and in 1948 he established an important new way of thinking about social influence.

TABLE 1

Percentage of Judgment Reversals by Condition*

	Linguistic	Ethical	Musical
Baseline	13	10	25
Majority	62	50	48
Experts	48	48	46

*From Moore (1921).

Asch, like Sherif and Lewin, had been strongly influenced by Gestalt psychology. Gestalt is the German word for "shape" or "form," and the thrust of Gestalt psychology is that psychological phenomena are organized, undivided, articulated forms. The form is something more than the summation of its parts, and the parts derive their properties from membership in the form. For example, combining several tones into a chord has a psychological effect that cannot be predicted from the sounds of the individual tones, and B flat in one chord has a different psychological effect than B flat in another chord.

Asch argued that Moore's explanation of judgmental conformity was too mechanistic and that it did not take into account the whole psychological form. His research was an attempt to illustrate the complexity of conformity.

Subjects were asked to rank ten professions (accountancy, business, dentistry, engineering, journalism, law, medicine, music, politics, teaching) for each of five qualities (intelligence, social usefulness, conscientiousness, stability of character, and idealism). At the time they were making their rankings, subjects had before them information indicating that 500 other college students had ranked politicians first in all respects or last in all respects. Subjects were heavily influenced by this information to rank politics either high or low. Moore would have expected such a result, but not Asch's explanation of it.

In order to determine why subjects were influenced, Asch questioned them after the ratings were made. When asked what particular group or groups of politicians they had in mind when making the judgments, those subjects who knew that other students had ranked politics high named such statesmen as Roosevelt, Hall, Stimson, and Norman Thomas. Those subjects who knew that the other students had rated politics low said they were describing caucus people, ward heelers, low politicians, the usual neighborhood politician, or Tammany Hall bosses.

From this evidence Asch argued that his subjects' judgmental conformity was not automatic and unconscious submission but rather thoughtful and conscious cooperation with the task at hand. Those subjects who knew that other students had rated politicians low among the professionals interpreted this as meaning that they should rank the more unsavory type of politician. If other students had rated politicians high, subjects thought that they should rate statesmen.

A catchy way to summarize this argument is that majority opinion determines, not the judgment of the object, but the object of the judgment.

Let us examine another application of the same argument. In an experiment by Lorge, published in 1936, subjects were asked to read the following passage: "I hold it that a little rebellion, now and then, is a good thing, and as necessary in the political world as storms are in the physical." If the statement were attributed to Thomas Jefferson, subjects tended to agree with it; if attributed to Lenin, to disagree with it. Lorge provided the apparently acceptable explanation that the prestige value of the author attached automatically to the statement and created the same emotional response to the statement as to the author.

Asch could not accept this explanation. In his view, the meaning of the statement was different when attributed to the two different authors. He repeated the experiment and asked subjects to write a short essay describing what they thought the state-ment meant. When describing the statement attributed to Lenin, the word "rebellion" meant revolution; when attributed to Jeffer-son, it meant peaceful change of political control. When the statement was attributed to Lenin, the word "little" was over-looked; when attributed to Jefferson, it was stressed. When inter-preting Lenin, subjects spoke of "letting loose of pent-up forces," of the need for action that "may be frightening and depressing at the time," of the necessity of "purging" the old order. When referring to Jefferson, they spoke of "new ideas in government and politics."

One might argue that Asch's subjects, by redefining the object to be judged in response to the ratings supposedly given by other people, were showing the same unreasoning conformity that Moore or Lorge attributed to their subjects. Asch would respond that a necessary part of rational life is to agree upon the object of judgment before judging it. Moore or Lorge might counter that Asch's subjects were merely rationalizing their con-formity by claiming to have changed the object of judgment. It was, and is, an interesting question.

5

Theodore Newcomb:
The Bennington Study, 1943

The decade of the 1930's produced the New Deal, the Spanish Civil War, labor unionism—many issues on which various people took markedly conservative or liberal positions. During this time, many people also changed from a conservative to a liberal posture. Newcomb, teaching at the newly-created Bennington College, decided to use the college itself as a natural laboratory to study the social and personality factors related to attitude change.

Newcomb reported his research in 1943 in *Personality and Social Change,* stating his central problem as follows: "What kind of personal characteristics, in any student community, determine those social relationships which in turn lead to varying reactions to proposed social changes? Such is the problem of this study" (p. 12).

Sherif had argued that one belongs to groups, that groups have norms, and that these norms influence the individual member's perceptions, attitudes, and personality. Newcomb believed, in addition, that one's personality determines the particular groups of which one becomes a member. Thus the process is circular, with personality and attitudes determining group membership and group membership influencing personality and attitude.

Bennington College was an ideal laboratory. For one thing it was a small school, and data could be collected from all of the

250 female students and the 50 faculty members. Secondly, because the girls were drawn from well-to-do families with quite conservative political and social values, while the young faculty members were intensely liberal, one could expect the students to show some change in values.

The campus was a town unto itself and was spoken of by students and faculty as "the community." The community was highly cohesive because of the small student body and the fact that there was no place to go except the small town of Bennington, four miles away. Cohesion was further enhanced by integrating freshmen into living groups with upperclassmen.

Prior to arriving at Bennington, the girls had been completely immersed in conservative political and economic beliefs. Their well-to-do parents resented social changes which reduced their privileged position in society. They believed that the concept of the "haves" being forced to share their rightful wealth with the "have-nots" was invented by the devil himself and could lead only to the destruction of capitalism. The girls heard this from their parents and eventually from their peers, who had been taught the same thing by their parents. The only disagreeing voice was an occasional courageous teacher.

Upon arriving at Bennington, the girls found that the authority figures, the faculty, held views that were in direct opposition to their own. And the sweet young things were ill-prepared to win arguments against the high-status and aggressive male intellectuals.

They also found the older students to be liberal. In classes, in bull sessions, and at meals, the girls heard liberal ideas presented and defended by fellow students, particularly those high in prestige. Parents were not often available to buttress the belief in the old ideas.

The degree of conflict experienced by the students between values of the community and the values of "back home" was nicely expressed in an essay written for an English course:

MORE THAN THE TUITION

It suddenly dawned on me that we'd never be able to go on like this, walking carefully around everything controversial, because everything controversial turned out to be all the vital things . . . After a while all the laughter and gaiety rang false—it was like a steady diet of waltzes and swing with never a symphony for serious times . . . Two years ago we agreed about everything, and we would have gotten married but I thought I wanted a degree . . . I don't want to go home this vacation—there's no one I want to see for more than 5 minutes.

An increasing crescendo of scattered remarks of my friends mounts up in my mind and culminates in a dissonant, minor chord. What is the matter with these dissatisfied, bewildered, cynical girls? It's a simple answer, yet dishearteningly complex. Bennington is their trouble. I can't speak for all of us, but a hell of a lot of us are in this fix. We come from fine old Tory families who believe firmly in Higher Education—God knows why. So they sent us to a well-spoken-of college with an interesting-sounding scheme of education. Mary Jane could pursue her interest at Bennington and not get a nervous breakdown over Math the way Mummie did at Wellesley. So we went to Bennington, and our friends went to Vassar, Yale, Sarah Lawrence, Harvard, finishing school, St. Paul's-to-broker's-office. They came home changed, a little. A slightly smarter jargon, unerring taste in clothes and Things To Do, and one and all, victrola records of the conventional ideas. We came home, some of us, talking a new language, some cobwebs swept out, a new direction opening up ahead we were dying to travel. Liberal, we thought we were. "What the hell's happened to you? Become a Parlor Pink?" "Well, hardly, ha, ha." It was a little bewildering. Oh, well, let's dance.

And then that fatal day came when we met The Man. God, but he's cute. And he likes us, and we have such a wonderful time together. Houseparties, football, dances, skiing, and laughter, laughter. It's love, all right. And Society approves, beamingly. Our backgrounds are the same and we meet our respective parents' ideals.

He's got a job now, and as soon as he's making enough we'll be married. We talk together about it a lot. We get a little more serious about what's ahead, and we start to talk soberly together for practically the first time. About all kinds of things. "We've known each other for such a long time now, but we've never had time to talk about this, Johnny—or this. What do you think about ——?" "Oh, come on, darling, let's have another drink—you'll get over it."

And we did get over it—with a jolt—but not what he thought. Sudden desperation—if I can't get along with Him—what the hell? To hell with Bennington? The more education, the broader-minded—and the narrower the circle of kindred souls. It's closing in on us now. Soon we'll graduate, and what then?

Back to the old "set" which we've outgrown. To people we can never be completely satisfied with again as friends, and who distrust us now, if we've been brave enough to show our colors. Most of us have played ball instead of that, and been hypocrites, with a sick feeling. Let's dance. Have another drink (Newcomb, 1943, pp. 11-12).

The writer of the essay had apparently accepted the liberal values of Bennington and had in the process become alienated from her family and friends outside the community. We would not expect all the girls to make that choice. Newcomb's task was to determine what forces caused some girls to choose Bennington and others to choose family and outside friends.

For several years, Newcomb administered a scale of Political and Economic Progressivism to the entire student body. A low score on this scale, indicating liberalism, would be obtained by an individual who favored a graduated income tax, unions, the right to strike, Social Security, a limit to business monopolies, and so forth. A high score indicated a desire to maintain or return to the political and economic system that existed prior to the Depression.

The scale was administered to one class for four consecutive years, to two other classes for three consecutive years, and to two additional classes for two consecutive years.

As shown in Figure 2, each class became more liberal with each year at Bennington.

This greater liberality was general rather than confined to specific issues. It was a philosophy rather than a set of parroted statements. The evidence for this is that when the Spanish Civil War suddenly became an issue, with little or no advance warning to the students, those who were least conservative regarding other issues immediately took the least conservative position toward this issue. The liberal position was, of course, to support Loyalist Spain against Franco.

Newcomb was not concerned, however, with demonstrating simply a general and lasting change in the student body as a whole. He wished to isolate the personal and social characteristics that might explain why some of the girls changed and others did not. To this end, Newcomb studied extensively the most conservative and least conservative sixths of three consecutive graduating classes.

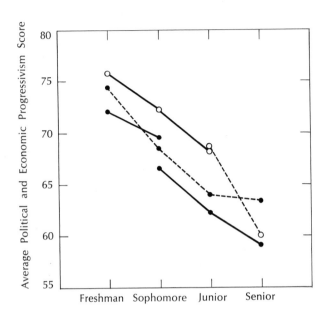

FIGURE 2.   Changes in Political and Economic Progressivism over
years at Bennington for five separate entering classes.
A low score indicates greater liberalism (Newcomb,
1943).

The most liberal girls were very popular, occupied leadership
positions, and were strongly identified with the Bennington community—being described by other students as "more absorbed in
college community affairs than anyone else in the class."

The most conservative girls, on the other hand, were described by other students as "indifferent to activities of student
committees" and as "resistant to community expectation regarding codes and standards." They tended to be the least popular
students, confining their social life to a small group of equally
conservative friends. In many cases, they were not even aware
that they were among the most conservative of Bennington students. Counselors and faculty members perceived them to be
overly dependent upon their parents.

We have, then, the following relationships: In a liberal college community, some students deviated from the community

values and remained conservative. These deviates tended to be rejected by their classmates (except for a small group of close friends) and tended to be unaware of the Bennington values.

What is cause and what is effect? There are three clear possibilities: (1) Deviation from the community values led to rejection by the community. (2) Some personal characteristic, such as physical appearance, led to rejection. The rejected girls did not become more liberal because their isolation prevented them from becoming aware of the Bennington values. (3) Some personal characteristic, such as over-dependency upon parents, led simultaneously to rejection by students (because over-dependency is unattractive) and to deviation (because over-dependent girls could not depart from parental values).

As in most correlational studies, as opposed to experimental studies, a decisive choice among these alternatives is impossible. One alternative may seem more reasonable than the others, but sometimes the most reasonable is the least true—particularly when dealing with human behavior. In later chapters we will encounter experimental approaches to the important phenomena demonstrated in the Bennington study.

As a final note, it may have occurred to you that those who became more liberal did so merely in order to achieve prestige in the college community and that they reverted to freshman conservatism after leaving the community. In order to check this possibility Newcomb interviewed a large number of the students almost 30 years later, in 1960. Newcomb found that these women were far less conservative in 1960 than would be expected in view of their demographic (income, age, etc.) characteristics. Furthermore, the women's husbands were more liberal than would be expected in view of their demographic characteristics. Thus, although liberalism might originally have been a function of striving after prestige in the college community, it became a lasting and autonomous value system.

6

Group Discussion and Social Change: Kurt Lewin

During the early years of the Second World War, the National Research Council asked Lewin and his students at the State University of Iowa for suggestions on persuading women to buy and serve visceral meats. A severe meat shortage existed, and the solution was to use the whole animal, including heart, sweetbreads, and kidneys. Always the theoretician, Lewin extended the reasoning used in the autocratic-democratic leadership study discussed in Chapter 3.

He reasoned that with regard to, say the serving of kidneys, there was for each individual a force field composed of driving and restraining forces. Perhaps women wanted something new to serve to their families, and they were attracted by the low cost of this type of meat, but they didn't know much about preparing kidneys and they were afraid that the family wouldn't eat them. Obviously, it would be necessary to increase the driving forces or to decrease the restraining forces acting on any one individual. Doing either should change the quasi-stationary equilibrium with regard to the serving of visceral meats.

But, Lewin theorized, changing the forces operating on an individual would not be enough to lead to lasting behavioral change. He argued that individual women are likely to be aware of how often other women use visceral meats. Since most individuals have learned to stay fairly close to the standards of the groups to which they belong or to which they wish to belong, the group level itself will serve to prevent behavioral change. The perception of a group standard creates additional driving and restraining forces designed to *maintain* the group level of behavior.

Any attempt to increase driving forces would result in the strengthening of the group-induced restraining forces. It is as if each individual's behavior is attached to the behavioral level of the group by a rubber band. Some divergence from the group level is permitted, but the further one moves from the group level, the stronger are the forces to return to that level.

In changing social habits such as the serving of visceral meats, then, the best strategy should be to change the group level rather than try to force the individual to depart from the group. According to Lewin, "as long as group values are unchanged, the individual will resist the changes more strongly the further he is to depart from the group standards. If the group standard itself is changed, the resistance which is due to the relation between individual and group standard is eliminated" (1951, p. 228). Changing the group standard would not only allow an individual to change her behavior, but would create forces directed toward change.

In order to determine the practicality of this reasoning, Lewin and his students compared the effectiveness of a procedure they called "group decision" with other techniques of influence.

In the first study of this series, the group decision technique was compared to a lecture (A. Bavelas, L. Festinger, P. Woodward, and A. Zander). Female Red Cross volunteers met in groups of 13 to 17. Half of the groups were given a lecture linking the use of visceral meats to the war effort and pointing out the favorable nutritional and economic factors in the use of these meats. The remaining groups engaged in a discussion led by an experienced group worker. He attempted to impart the same information contained in the lecture and to remove any doubts expressed. In addition, he persuaded 100 per cent of the women to raise their hands indicating that they would serve visceral meats in the near future. He also promised to talk to each woman later to find out whether she had served the meats.

Only 3 per cent of the lecture subjects served visceral meats in the next few weeks; 32 per cent of the group decision subjects did so.

The group decision procedure clearly differed in several
ways from the lecture condition. The group decision subjects discussed the issue, made a unanimous public decision, and expected
a follow-up interview; none of this was true for the lecture subjects. Another potentially important difference was that the lecturer and the group leader were different people. The lecturer
was a female, while the group leader was Alex Bavelas, sometimes known as the Tyrone Power of social psychology. The
charm of Bavelas might have accounted for the results entirely.

In the next study in the series (M. Radke and D. Klisurich,
1947) the same person served as lecturer and as group leader.
Housewives in groups ranging from six to nine members were
urged to serve more milk to their families. Again the group decision procedure proved far more effective than the lecture. This
indicated not only that Bavelas was not necessary, but also that it
was not necessary for the group members to be part of a perma-
nent and organized group (as were the Red Cross workers).

One very plausible explanation for the effectiveness of group
decision could be that each person received individual attention
and had a chance to have her questions answered. In order to
rule out this explanation, the next experiment compared group
decision to individual instruction (M. Radke and D. Klisurich,
1947). Individual instruction was simply a conversation in which
a woman was urged to serve more orange juice and cod liver oil
to her children. Once again, group decision was the more effective technique. The experiment also demonstrated that the group
members needn't know one another at all; subjects were women
who lived in different places and simply attended the same clinic.

While these studies have ruled out some of the possible
explanations for the effectiveness of group decision, there are still
several ways in which the lecture and group decision conditions
differed. The group decisions always yielded a 100 per cent positive decision which the women made publicly, and the group
members expected a follow-up within a short period of time.
None of this was true for the lecture groups. After Lewin's death,
Edith Bennett attempted to isolate the particular factor which
really made the difference.

Miss Bennett used either a lecture or a group discussion
(each with 8 to 16 students per group) to raise the willingness of
University of Michigan students to volunteer as experimental sub-

jects. The dependent variable was whether or not the students later went to a "central file" and made their names and telephone numbers available.

In addition to the type of influence attempt (lecture vs. group decision vs. no influence attempt), the commitment level was also varied. In a "no decision condition," students were dismissed after the influence attempt. In an "anonymous decision condition," students wrote anonymous statements about their willingness to volunteer. In a "partially anonymous decision condition," students raised their hands to indicate their willingness to volunteer; and in a "public commitment condition," students raised their hands and gave their names to the experimenter, who openly recorded them.

In no condition did the students know that a "central file" was to be established until after the influence attempt and the commitment. That is, they did not expect a follow-up. Any obtained difference between lecture and group decision groups could not be due to some group expecting a follow-up while other groups did not. Nor could any obtained difference be due to asking for public decisions in the group decision condition, because public decisions were also required in some of the lecture groups.

In fact, there were no differences between lecture and group decision in percentage of students going to the central file. About one in five in each condition did go. Nor did it make any difference whether the decision was anonymous, partially anonymous, or public. These conditions, however, were uniformly higher in producing action than the no decision condition. It would appear then that Lewin's results might have been due partially to asking group decision subjects to make a decision and not asking this of the lecture subjects.

This could not have been the entire explanation, however, because the differences Bennett found between decision and no decision subjects were much smaller than those found by Lewin between group decision and lecture.

In order to provide a fuller explanation, Bennett gave the students in the experiment a questionnaire a week after the closing of the central file. The important question for this discussion was, How many from your group would you estimate signed up with the central file?

Following Lewin's theorizing about group standards, Bennett reasoned that those students who perceived that many of their fellow group members had acted would be more likely to have acted themselves. This turned out to be the case, at least in those groups in which, *objectively,* there were many positive decisions to act. In 10 of the 13 groups having the highest percentage of positive decisions (whether anonymous or public), those students who perceived that many positive decisions had been made were most likely to act.

Bennett's clinching analysis was to compare those subjects most like the Lewinian group decision subjects to those most like his lecture subjects.

Subjects most like Lewin's group decision participants were those who had been asked to make a decision and themselves decided to volunteer in the setting of a group in which a high proportion of positive decisions had been indicated. Bennett found that 34 per cent of these students acted. Subjects most like Lewin's lecture participants were those who had been asked to make no decision at all. Among Bennett's subjects, only 15 per cent acted. This difference is approximately of the same magnitude as that obtained by Lewin.

In summary, Bennett's results suggest that group discussion itself is not important in effecting behavioral change or action. But as Lewin originally theorized, it is important that the group member make a positive decision and that he perceive that other group members have also made positive decisions. Changing the group standard both removes forces opposing change and creates forces toward establishing and maintaining a new group level.

Leon Festinger:
Theory of Informal Social
Communication, 1950

Festinger was a student of Kurt Lewin, had participated in the group decision research, and was strongly influenced by Lewin's insistence on a general theoretical approach. The Theory of Informal Social Communication is the first real "theory" to be considered in this book. Concepts are defined and related to one another, and specific testable predictions are derived.

Festinger was concerned with the communication process in informal groups: why do people talk, to whom do they talk, what is the result of their talking? He chose to concentrate on the tendency of people to try to reach agreement in groups. He assumed that there were two reasons for pressures toward uniformity of opinion to exist within a group.

One of these reasons is the need for *group locomotion*. If a group has a goal and if it is necessary for all of the members of the group to hold similar opinions in order for the group to move toward that goal, pressures toward uniformity will exist.

The second and more important reason is the need for *social reality*. In Festinger's words:

> . . . if a discrepancy in opinion, attitude, or belief exists among persons who are members of an appropriate reference group, forces to communicate will arise. It also follows that the less

"physical reality" there is to validate the opinion or belief, the greater will be the importance of the social referent, the group, and the greater will be the forces to communicate (Festinger, 1950, p. 273).

There is a dimension of reality which at one end is based entirely upon physical evidence and at the other relies completely upon social consensus. Whether a piece of glass is fragile or not is a question of physical reality. The question can be answered simply by smashing the glass with a hammer. Whether one candidate would have been a better president than another is, however, impossible to determine by physical means. One can examine the campaign promises of both candidates and the presidential record of the winner as well as the expert opinions of historians, political scientists, and the like. But one can never answer the question conclusively in one way or another. One will be fairly confident of the accuracy of his opinion if all of his friends agree with him—they thus provide social reality.

Although each member of a group wants his confidence in the accuracy of his opinions to be enhanced through agreement with others, mere agreement is not enough; agreement must be reached fairly. If all members of a group decided to flip a coin to determine who would have been the best president, and then to agree on whichever candidate the coin elected, agreement would not create confidence. Agreement is related to confidence only if each individual reaches an opinion independently on evidence he finds compelling. Then agreement with others gives him some confidence in his assumptions and his reasoning. This does not mean that the individual will not try to influence the opinions of others. On the contrary, the more effective he is in changing the opinions of others, the more he will feel that his assumptions and logic are compelling. He must believe, however, that the others change their opinions because of the intrinsic value of his argument, and not out of a mere desire to please him.

The pressures to uniformity created by the need for group locomotion and the need for social reality are presumed to act upon the group in exactly the same way.

Festinger and his associates suggested three variables which they thought would affect the strength of the pressures toward uniformity:

(1) *Opinion discrepancy within the group.*   The greater the opinion discrepancy within a group, the stronger the pressures toward uniformity. It is quite obvious that if there is no opinion discrepancy within a group there can be no pressures toward uniformity. How can there be pressures toward a state of affairs which already exists? According to the theory, uniformity of opinion is desired by the group members; and the further the group moves from this desired state of affairs, the stronger are the forces to reduce opinion discrepancy. Festinger implies that there is no limit to the relationship between opinion discrepancy and pressures toward uniformity. It may be, however, that if opinion discrepancy becomes great enough, pressures toward uniformity will be reduced; group members would perceive the impossibility of opinion homogeneity.

(2) *Relevance to group.*   To the extent that an opinion, attitude, or a belief is relevant to the group, pressures toward uniformity will be high. Relevance is difficult to define. In some sense, anything the group discusses is relevant to the group; but in another sense, some things are clearly more relevant to a group than others. It is relevant to a Friday night poker group to bet on who will win an upcoming election; it is far less relevant to such a group to agree upon the best candidate. But the latter question is of great relevance to a political group which must make a recommendation to others.

(3) *Group cohesiveness.*   Cohesiveness is defined as the *resultant* of all the forces acting upon the individual to remain in the group. The group may be highly cohesive because the members have pleasant outgoing personalities, because the members have interests in common, because the group provides individuals the opportunity to engage in certain behaviors or accomplish certain ends, because belonging to the group provides status to the individual, or because of any number of other things.
There are also reasons not to belong to a group. The group may meet at inconvenient times, it may include unattractive or disagreeable individuals, it may require too much time and money, or there may be more attractive groups one could join if one weren't a member of this group. If we subtract all of the

forces pointing away from group membership from those forces pointing toward group membership, we have cohesiveness.

Festinger hypothesized that the greater the cohesiveness of a group, the greater the pressures toward uniformity within that group. It is by no means obvious that cohesiveness should increase the pressures toward uniformity, and Festinger did not attempt to explain why this should be the case. Indeed, one might guess intuitively that a highly cohesive group could tolerate differences of opinion. Perhaps it is that members of a cohesive group feel or come to feel that they are similar to one another in important ways. Any dissimilarity of opinion or belief would then be jarringly inconsistent with the general feeling of similarity. Or it could be that members of a cohesive group come to like one another a great deal, and the human animal finds it inconceivable that a person he likes could possibly disagree with him! We have now examined the three variables which determine the strength of pressures toward uniformity. Pressure toward uniformity is in itself an invisible, hypothetical construct. What does it cause members to do that we can measure and see? Festinger suggested three behavioral manifestations of pressures toward uniformity, each of them designed to reduce opinion discrepancy within the group. In shorthand form these are *change other, change self,* or *reject other.*

(1) *Change Other.* The first thing an individual tries to do is to change others within the group so that they come to agree with him. The individual will initiate argument with that person in the group who is most dissimilar in opinion. But there are two exceptions to this rule. A person will not initiate an argument with someone he knows he can't change, and he will not argue with someone who is seen as an undesirable member of the group. If after a period of argument, the other has not changed his opinion, our zealous advocate will cease arguing because it no longer seems likely that the other can be changed.

(2) *Change Self.* If the individual cannot change other group members so that they agree with him he may change his own opinion. Given strong pressures to uniformity, the major determinants of whether an individual will change his opinion upon receiving a persuasive communication are the extent to

which the individual is attracted to the group, and the confidence he has in his own opinion. Man is a rigid animal, and changing one's opinion hurts. If belonging to the group is not particularly important or attractive, and if the individual is very confident, it may be easier for him to leave the group than to change his opinion.

(3) *Reject Other.* Festinger referred to this process as "changing the composition of the group," but it is simpler to think of it as rejecting others. Suppose that an individual has tried diligently but unsuccessfully to change the other. Suppose, further, that he is unwilling to change his own opinion because that would move him away from others in the group who already agree with him. And, finally, the individual is highly attracted to the group and does not wish to leave it. What can be done to achieve uniformity within the group? The individual may redefine the group either actually or psychologically in such a way as to exclude the deviate other. If he has sufficient power and influence within the group he may work to have the other physically rejected from the group. If that is not possible he may psychologically reject the other by saying, "There is no way to get rid of that fellow but as far as I am concerned he doesn't really belong in this group, and I am not going to be bothered by his stupid opinions." The more extreme the discrepancy of opinion between self and other, the stronger will be the tendency to reject the other.

That is the essence of Festinger's theory of informal social communication. It is a nice theory—clear, elegantly simple, and eminently testable.

Perhaps the most comprehensive test of any portion of the theory was done by Stanley Schachter (1951), a colleague of Festinger. Schachter's subjects were college students who had volunteered to be members of continuing clubs. There were four types of clubs: case study, editorial, movie, and radio. The clubs were described to students, who then indicated how interested they were in joining particular clubs. The case study and movie clubs were composed of those students who had indicated a high degree of interest in belonging to such a group; these were the *High Cohesive* groups. Editorial and radio clubs were composed of individuals who had indicated little interest in belonging to such clubs; these were the *Low Cohesive* groups. Cohesiveness was thus determined by the attractiveness of the club activities to the members.

At the first meeting of each club subjects were asked to read a short version of the "Johnny Rocco" case. This was the life history of a juvenile delinquent awaiting sentence for a minor crime. Each club was asked to discuss and decide the question, What should be done with this kid? the discussion being guided by a seven point scale ranging from the "give him love and understanding" viewpoint to the "punish him severely" viewpoint. The case was written in such a way that nearly all subjects chose a scale position toward the love and kindness end of the continuum. After the five to seven naive group members had announced their scale positions on the case study, the three confederates of the experimenter who were posing as group members announced their position. The first confederate, whom we will call the "mode," announced a position very much in agreement with the naive subjects. The second confederate, the "slider," announced an extremely harsh position on the scale and during the course of the conversation allowed himself to be persuaded by the group members to move toward their positions. The third confederate was the "deviate"; he took an extremely harsh position toward Johnny Rocco and maintained it through the ensuing discussion.

In order to test another portion of Festinger's theory, relevance of the case study to the group was also manipulated. The case study was obviously *Relevant* to the case study clubs, and it was made *Relevant* to the editorial clubs by the experimenter's statement that the case was part of a feature article on juvenile delinquency. The case study was made *Irrelevant* to the radio and movie clubs by the experimenter's statement that the writer of the case simply wanted the opinions of some other people.

During the forty-five minute discussion an observer noted who spoke to whom and for what period of time. The experimental confederates responded to any communication addressed to them with simply a restatement of the position they were holding at the time. If no communication was addressed to a confederate within a five-minute period, he initiated one.

At the end of the discussion two measures of rejection were taken. The first was committee nominations. Each subject had to suggest each of the other group members for one of three committees: the executive committee, the steering committee, or the correspondence committee. The first two committees were described as fairly important, while the correspondence committee was merely to perform tedious secretarial functions. Thus a nomination to the correspondence committee was taken as an indication of rejection. The second measure was a sociometric test. Subjects were told that it might be necessary to reduce the size of the group and therefore they were to rank everyone present in terms of how much they would like for them to remain in the group. A low ranking indicated rejection.

In summary the experiment contained four conditions: *High Cohesive—Relevant, High Cohesive—Irrelevant, Low Cohesive—Relevant* and *Low Cohesive—Irrelevant.* Pressures toward uniformity should be especially strong in the first of the four conditions and very weak in the last of the conditions. This is because of the theoretical statement that both high cohesiveness and relevance increase pressures toward uniformity. The theory also states that pressures toward uniformity are strongest when there is a large discrepancy between two people. Thus we would expect subjects in this experiment, particularly in the *High Cohesive—Relevant* condition, to attempt to reduce the discrepancy between themselves and the deviate. Because each subject provides support for the other subjects, we would not expect individuals in this experiment to change their own opinions. Rather, we would expect them to attempt to change the deviate's opinion and failing that, to reject him.

This situation is an experimental analogue of what Newcomb observed at Bennington College. The Bennington community was highly cohesive, and the issue of political and economic liberalism was highly relevant. Furthermore, deviates from the liberal atmosphere of the college were unpopular. The data from Bennington did not, however, allow us to draw firm conclusions about the direction of causation in the relationship between deviation and rejection by classmates.

In Schachter's experiment, each confederate played the role of deviate, slider, and mode equally often; thus if only the deviate is rejected, we may conclude that deviation *per se* leads to rejection.

The results were generally in line with predictions. There were many more communications addressed to the deviate than to either the mode or the slider. Furthermore, there were more communications to the slider than to the mode, particularly during the early part of discussion before the slider had changed his position. In three of the conditions, communications to the deviate increased throughout the forty-five minute discussion period. Only in the *High Cohesive—Relevant* condition did communications to the deviate decrease toward the end of the discussion session. This decrease in communication to the deviate was interpreted by Schachter as an indication that the deviate was being rejected. And the *High Cohesiveness—Relevant* condition, where pressures to uniformity were the greatest, is precisely where rejection of the deviate should first occur. Had the discussion lasted for a longer period of time, we would expect a total cessation of communication to the deviate in the *High Cohesive —Relevant* condition. We would also expect subjects in the other three conditions to eventually reduce the frequency of communications to the deviate.

Evidence collected after the discussion also indicated that participants in the role of the deviate were rejected, while these same participants in the role of the slider or the mode in other groups were not rejected. On the sociometric test, subjects were asked to rank the other group members according to how much they would like for them to remain in the group. In all conditions the deviate was ranked as a less desirable group member than either the mode or the slider. The theory would predict that because pressures toward uniformity are greater in the *High Cohesive* conditions than in the *Low Cohesive* conditions, the deviate should be more soundly rejected by the *High Cohesive* subjects. The data strongly confirmed this prediction. For reasons which are unclear, the data did not confirm the prediction from the theory that the deviate should be more strongly rejected by the *Relevant* groups than by the *Irrelevant* groups. Finally, those subjects in the *High Cohesive—Relevant* groups who most markedly decreased communication to the deviate during the discussion also were the subjects who afterward rated him least desirable as a group member. This supports Schachter's interpretation that reduction in communication to a deviate indicated rejection.

Data from the post-discussion committee nominations also tended to support the theory. The deviate was consistently over-nominated for the least important committee, the correspondence committee. Furthermore, he was nominated to this committee more frequently by the *Relevant* groups than by the *Irrelevant* groups. Thus, while the *High Cohesive* groups indicated their rejection of the deviate by ranking him an undesirable group member, the *Relevant* groups indicated their rejection by nominating the deviate for the least important of the three committees.

Because Schachter's deviate was an experimental confederate, the experiment tells us nothing about the behavior of deviate members of a group. Does increasing the cohesiveness of a group increase the tendency of deviate members to try to change the opinions of those who disagree with them the most? Or does increasing the cohesiveness increase the deviate's tendency to change his own opinion? Are both of these tendencies increased equally by an increase in cohesiveness? In order to answer questions such as these and additional questions relevant to basic assumptions of the theory, an ambitious experiment was done by Festinger, Gerard, Hymovitch, Kelley, and Raven (1952).

Groups of six to nine males or females met in the laboratory and were told that they were to study a case history of a labor dispute and then discuss it via written messages. Four variables were manipulated:

(1) *Cohesiveness.* Subjects in the *High Cohesive* condition were told that they had very similar interests and backgrounds and should be very compatible. Subjects in the *Low Cohesive* condition were told that, due to scheduling difficulties, the experimenters had not been able to bring together people who had very much in common. To strengthen the difference between *High* and *Low Cohesive* groups, subjects were asked to write "get acquainted" notes to one another. Each subject made three copies of a note, with the notes to be distributed randomly to three other group members. Actually, the experimenters collected the notes and substituted notes they had prepared ahead of time. The fake notes in the *High Cohesive* condition expressed enthusiasm and congeniality. Notes in the *Low Cohesive* condition expressed some doubt about the composition of the group and the meaning of the task.

(2) *Presence or Absence of Experts.* Subjects in the *Expert Present* condition were told that the group included some individuals who had had special training and experience with labor

relations problems. Subjects in the *Expert Absent* condition were told that all members of the group had approximately equal experience and knowledge about labor relations problems.

(3) *Presence or Absence of a Correct Answer.* Subjects were to make a prediction from the case history about how the union members would behave in negotiations that took place at a later time. They were to make these predictions on a seven-point scale ranging from "they will be defiant and insolent in pressing for their demands, totally resistant to compromise proposals, and determined to hold out indefinitely for all of their demands" to "they will comply with the counter-proposals at the beginning of the meeting, immediately making the necessary concessions in order to reach agreement." In the *Correct Answer* condition subjects were told that after the discussion they would be informed as to how the union members actually did behave. In the *No Correct Answer* condition subjects were told that prior to final negotiations the federal government stepped in and imposed a solution. Thus no one was sure how the union members would have behaved.

(4) *Deviate versus Conformer.* After subjects had read the case history, each privately chose one of the statements on the seven-point scale. The experimenter collected the scales, tabulated them, and gave to each subject separately the tabulation showing the opinion of each of the other group members. Some of the subjects were made to feel that they *Conformed* to the group opinion. Their tabulation indicated that one person was three steps away on the seven-point scale, that one or two other individuals were one step away, and that the remainder of the group members (three to five people) were at exactly the same point as the subject on the scale. Other subjects were made to feel like *Deviates*. They were told that one or two subjects were two steps away and that the remaining subjects in the group (four to six people) were three steps away.

After receiving this feedback about the opinions of the other group members, subjects were asked to state their opinion again privately. In this way the strength of the tendency to change self could be measured. Immediately after this second opinion measure, subjects were asked to spend several minutes writing as many notes as they wanted to other group members. These notes were to be collected and distributed to the appropriate recipients at a later time. During this period no subject received any notes, but each of them wrote several. The number of words written to people at different positions on the scale provided a measure of the strength of the tendency to change others. The messages also provided a measure of the strength of the tendency to redefine the boundaries of a group (or to reject those group members whose opinions were most different from one's own).

The results of this experiment are very complex, and they will be summarized in general terms with an attempt to relate them to the theory.

The theory states that ". . . the less physical reality there is to validate the opinion or belief, the greater will be the importance of the social referent, the group, and the greater will be the forces to communicate" (Festinger et al., 1952, p. 345). The investigators reasoned that when subjects believed there was an expert in the group, or when they believed they would be told the correct answer after the discussion, there would be less dependence upon the group itself to validate the opinion. Thus, the pressures toward uniformity of opinion should be less. The data tended to support this prediction. When subjects believed they would learn the correct answer later, or when they believed there was an expert in the group, changes in opinion were observed, but the other two manifestations of the process—influencing others and redefining the boundaries of the group—were less common.

One manifestation of the pressure toward uniformity is a tendency to change one's own opinion to become more like that of other group members. Since the Conformer was already in agreement with the majority of group members, we would expect his tendency to change his own opinion to be far less than that of the Deviate. This was indeed the case, with 23 per cent of the Deviates changing their opinions after seeing the distribution of opinions in the group, while only 4 per cent of the Conformers changed their opinions.

Because pressures toward uniformity should have been higher in the High Cohesive groups, we would expect Deviates in these conditions to change their opinions more often than Deviates in the Low Cohesive conditions. There was a slight difference in the expected direction, with 26 per cent of the *High Cohesive Deviates* changing and only 18 per cent of the *Low Cohesive Deviates* changing.

The second manifestation of pressures toward uniformity is the tendency to communicate to and influence group members who disagree. Thus, theoretically, we would expect individuals to address most of their communications to those people who were most in disagreement with them, and we would expect this tendency to be greater under *High Cohesive* than under *Low Cohesive* conditions. Table 2 presents the relevant data, the average number of words written to each person at each position by *Deviates* and *Conformers* in *High* and *Low Cohesive* conditions. Looking first at the *Conformers,* it is apparent that most of their communications were addressed to the most extreme deviate, indicating strong attempts at influence.

TABLE 2

Average Number of Words Written to Each
Person at Each Position*

| Opinion of recipient | Conformer | | Deviate | |
Cohesiveness	High	Low	High	Low
3 steps removed	40	44	13	11
2 steps removed	—	—	20	13
1 step removed	18	18	—	—
0 steps removed	5	3	—	—

*From Festinger, Gerard, Hymovitch, Kelley, and Raven (1952).

The predicted difference (in number of notes addressed to the *Deviate)* between *High* and *Low Cohesiveness* did not develop. While this does not confirm the theory, neither does it disconfirm it. One could argue that even with the *Low Cohesive* manipulation, finding oneself in agreement with most of the group members in itself increased cohesiveness among *Conformers* to about as high a level as is possible.

Among the *Deviates,* there was a difference between *High* and *Low Cohesive* groups with the *High Cohesive Deviates* making more influence attempts. However, both groups of *Deviates* communicated more times to the one or two individuals two steps removed than to the four to six people three steps removed.

This may be taken as evidence that the *Deviates* were redefining the boundaries of the group by rejecting the group members who were most in disagreement with them. The fact that the *High Cohesive Deviates* showed a stronger tendency to reject than the *Low Cohesive Deviates* is quite consistent with the theory. From these results the investigators formulated another theoretical statement, "The relative strength of the tendency to redefine the boundaries of the group in response to pressures toward uniformity increases for a member as the discrepancy between his opinion and the modal opinion in the group increases" (Festinger et al., 1952, p. 345).

In summary, *Deviates* exceeded *Conformers* in changing their own opinions and in redefining the boundaries of the group. *Deviates* and *Conformers* were approximately equal in the number of words written to influence others. Thus, if we take into account all three manifestations of pressures toward uniformity, *Deviates* appear to have experienced the stronger pressures toward uniformity. This is very reasonable if one assumes greater opinion discrepancy in the group from the *Deviate* point of view than from the *Conformer* point of view.

Several other experiments have been conducted to test certain aspects of Festinger's theory, and most results have been consistent with the predictions. In a later chapter a newer and broader formulation of this same position will be discussed.

8

The Asch Effect: 1951

I have mentioned previously Asch's strong emphasis on man's rationality. After encountering Sherif's research on the formation of perceptual norms in the auto-kinetic situation, Asch reasoned that the norm formation could have occurred in one of two different ways: (1) The effect was a result of automatic mutual imitation, or an expression of suggestibility. (2) The effect was a result of a rational response to a situation in which two or more people are making a perceptual judgment about the same object.

Asch favored the second alternative and thought that a subject in the auto-kinetic situation may have reasoned as follows:

> My partner and I ought to be in agreement about this judgment we are making, but for some reason he is reporting more movement than I am. Maybe if I turn my head slightly and don't look at the light so directly I'll see it more like he does. Ah, that's better! And his judgment wasn't as large that time as before. So we both must be approaching an accurate judgment. Also I think maybe I've been underestimating how long an inch is—it's very hard to tell when you can't see anything to compare with.

In other words, Asch believed that Sherif's subjects did a great deal of cognitive work in order to achieve a perceptual agreement they considered to be logically necessary. Sherif had not, however, questioned his subjects extensively about their experiences and feelings in the auto-kinetic situation. Asch began his research with the intention of understanding the subjects' states of mind during the experimental session. Asch, in short, was somewhat more concerned with the process of social influence as it occurred; Sherif was more interested in the product of social influence as that product operated in solitary judgmental sessions.

Another important difference was in the experimental situations employed. Sherif used a completely ambiguous judgment and concluded that norms arise under conditions of ambiguity. Asch used a totally unambiguous judgment in order to produce clear and dramatic psychological states in his subjects.

The basic Asch situation was quite simple. Seven to nine individuals were brought together to take part in "an experiment in visual discrimination." They were instructed to match the length of a standard line with one of three comparison lines, and to announce their judgments in the order in which they were seated. The single naive subject was seated in the next to the last seat, and the other group members had been instructed previously to respond on certain trials with wrong judgments. Thus on every trial the subject was faced with a very clear perceptual judgment; it was apparent that comparison line A, for example, was the same length as the standard line. But on some trials the first group member said that comparison line C, for example, was the same as the standard. This was very surprising to the subject because comparison line C was anywhere from ¾ to 1¾ inches different in length from the standard line. The subject was even more puzzled when the second group member also said that comparison line C was the correct judgment. When it was finally the subject's turn to make his own judgment he had heard every single group member answering before him choose comparison line C as the correct answer. He had no reason to believe that all the other group members were blind or that they were not motivated to make the correct judgment. Yet his visual impression was unmistakable—comparison line A was the correct answer. Regardless of what the subject decided to do, the other members of the group behaved impersonally and did not indicate any surprise at any answer he gave. The experimenter also behaved in a formal and impersonal manner.

How did the subjects deal with this impossible situation? Asch found that subjects resisted group influence on about two-thirds of the critical trials. There were strong individual differences; about one-fourth of the subjects made no errors at all, and another one-third agreed with the group on half or more of the trials.

In further experimental variations, Asch discovered additional aspects of the conformity process.

In one experimental variation, it was arranged that the subject arrived after the other group members had already started on the judgment task. In order that the ongoing task not be interrupted, the subject was asked to write down his judgment on each trial rather than speaking it aloud. This greatly reduced conformity; about two-thirds of the conformity errors made under public conditions disappeared. This impressive finding indicates that most of the conformity was due to fear of the opinions or reactions of the other group members.

On some critical trials in the public condition, the standard line was the same length as the shortest of the three comparison lines, while the group chose the longest of the three. Under these conditions, subjects frequently compromised between their own perception and that of the group, choosing the middle length of the three lines. This supported Asch's belief in a conscious attempt at accommodation, as opposed to blind imitation.

On some of the critical trials, the three comparison lines were much more similar to one another in length than on other trials. The more similar they were, the greater the conformity. Ambiguity is the mother of conformity.

If the "group" consisted of only one person other than the subject, there was very little conformity. Adding a second person increased conformity, and adding a third person increased it markedly. Further additions to the group (up to nine) had no effect. This curious result has no convincing explanation.

In some groups, one of the experimental confederates was instructed to give the correct response on some of the critical trials. Regardless of how many group members gave the wrong response, the subject rarely conformed. Perhaps having a partner removed the subject's fear of the group's reaction. Or perhaps the partner shamed the subject into reporting what he actually saw. Subjects tended to adopt a psychological set early in the experiment and behave consistently throughout the experiment. Those subjects who yielded to the majority early in the experiment continued to yield; those who resisted the majority continued to resist.

Asch questioned his subjects about the sets they adopted and concluded that each subject had one of three responses to the situation: to be honest, to be accurate, or to be socially acceptable.

Those who adopted the honesty set did not yield. They interpreted their task as reporting what they saw, whether correct or incorrect. A subject with this set might have been convinced that the group was correct, but he would nevertheless not conform.

Those subjects who adopted a social acceptance set were not concerned with whether they were accurate or not. They decided to give responses which would not make them stand out from the other members of the group. They didn't want other group members to laugh at them or to think them odd, nor did they want the experimenter to direct his attention at them. Such a motivation is undoubtedly a product of past experiences in which the individual has experienced unpleasant consequences as a result of standing out from others. These are the subjects one would expect to be more independent in the experimental variation in which they were allowed to write down their judgments rather than speaking them aloud.

Those subjects who adopted the accuracy set believed that they should give the response which, taking everything into consideration, they believed to be correct. Such a subject had to weigh his belief in the accuracy of his own perception against his belief in the accuracy of the perception of other people. Both sources of information, one's own perceptions and the perceptions of others, are trustworthy sources of information and are generally in agreement. If the individual believed the shortest line to be correct, and if the group gave as its judgment the longest line, the subject could combine the two sources of information by choosing the middle line as the correct judgment. If, however, the subject perceived the middle length line as being correct and the group named either of the other two comparison lines as its judgment, compromise judgment was impossible. In this case, the individual had to give his own judgment either more or less weight than the majority judgment, which would produce either independence or yielding respectively.

Asch stressed the rationality of the accuracy set. He wrote that "not to take it (the group) into account, not to allow one's self to be in any way affected by it, would be willful" (Asch, 1952, p. 484). Information from other people is normally trustworthy, and intelligent people should take it into account along with information from their own senses.

Unfortunately, there is a flaw in Asch's conclusion that a number of subjects acted "rationally" and adopted an accuracy set. The flaw is that when subjects gave their judgments privately (by writing them rather than speaking them aloud), there was very little conformity. When judgments were given publicly, the average number of errors was 4.4; when judgments were given privately, the average number of errors was only 1.5 (out of 12 possible). It would appear then that there was little tendency to consider the judgment of the majority trustworthy. Most of the conformity was due to fear of being different publicly and to fear of ridicule.

Social psychologists today distinguish between public compliance and private acceptance of social influence. Most of the effect obtained by Asch was public compliance. Sherif, on the other hand, obtained public compliance and private acceptance; even when they were no longer in the presence of their partner, subjects continued to judge the auto-kinetic movement according to the frame of reference established with their partner. It appears that private acceptance of social influence on perceptual judgment is limited to situations in which the stimulus conditions are ambiguous.

9

Leon Festinger: Theory of Social Comparison Processes

Social Comparison Theory (SCT) was a very ambitious attempt to explain various aspects of social behavior with a completely non-social motivation. As it was an extension of Festinger's earlier Theory of Informal Social Communication but differed in basic orientation, let us review the earlier theory.

It began with the premise that pressures toward uniformity of opinion existed in groups. These pressures have two sources: (1) Groups have goals and it is sometimes necessary for the members of a group to have similar opinions in order for the group to move toward the goal, and (2) If there is no physical reality against which to validate an opinion, pressures arise within the group to produce social reality through agreement. Pressures toward uniformity are strong to the extent that the group is cohesive, the opinion is relevant to the group, and there is opinion discrepancy within the group. Uniformity is achieved by changing the opinions of others, changing one's own opinion, or psychologically redefining the boundaries of the group to exclude those who disagree.

SCT was stated in the form of numerous hypotheses, corollaries, and derivations which need not be reproduced here. The major points are as follows:

1. *There is a drive in the human organism to hold correct opinions about the world and to have an accurate appraisal of one's abilities.* This states a non-social motivation upon which the remainder of the theory is constructed. It is based on the assumption that if humans did not have such a drive they could not survive. ". . . to have an accurate appraisal of one's abilities" means to know how good one is and what one can do in the world.

2. *To the extent that objective, non-social means are not available, people evaluate their opinions and abilities by comparison respectively with the opinions and abilities of others.*

3. *Given a range of possible persons for comparison, someone who ought to be close to one's own ability or opinion will be chosen for comparison.*

4. *When a discrepancy exists with respect to opinions or abilities there will be tendencies to change one's own position so as to move closer to others in the group, or to change others in the group to bring them closer to oneself, or to cease comparing oneself with those in the group who are very different from oneself.* Point 3 states that we will choose to compare with someone whom we think will be similar to ourselves. Point 4 states that if we make a mistake and choose a dissimilar comparison person, we will attempt to create similarity. Failing that, we will cease comparison.

5. *Pressures to uniformity concerning an opinion or an ability increase with the importance of the opinion or ability, its relevance to immediate behavior, one's attraction to the group, and the relevance to the group of the opinion or ability.*

6. *If persons who are very divergent from one's own opinion or ability are perceived as different from oneself on attributes consistent with the divergence, the tendency to narrow the range of comparability becomes stronger.* Point 4 states that if we cannot create similarity with a comparison person, there will be a tendency to cease comparing ourselves to that person. Point 6 states that the tendency becomes stronger if we can find some reason why the comparison person ought to be dissimilar. For example, a former tennis champion has an attribute (experience and practice) which is consistent with the divergence in our current tennis skills; I would cease comparing my ability to his.

7. *There is a unidirectional drive upward in the case of abilities but not in the case of opinions.* Having the same opinion as others creates confidence in that opinion, but having somewhat more skill than others produces a feeling of confidence.

Other than the fact that SCT deals with abilities as well as opinions, the major difference between the theories is that the early theory stressed the power of the group over the individual, while SCT stresses the individual using other people in order to fulfill his own needs. For example, pressures toward uniformity were increased in the earlier theory by the cohesiveness of the group; in SCT they are increased by the individual's attraction to the group.

This difference in basic orientation does not make the theories inconsistent with one another, however, and the experiments supporting the Theory of Informal Social Communication also support SCT. SCT does have the advantage of suggesting why we might or might not join certain groups and how we might be affected by individuals who are not in a face-to-face group with us. Hopefully, these points will be clearly understood after a close examination of SCT.

Assume that I believe that marijuana should be legalized. As a human organism, it is important to me that my opinion be correct. But, although I know some facts about marijuana that suggest it is far less harmful than alcohol, there can be no physical evidence that it *ought* to be legalized. Whether one thinks the law ought to be changed or not depends upon one's values and one's predictions of possible consequences. Given that I cannot find physical reality for the correctness of my opinion, I must seek social reality. How do I go about it?

According to SCT I would compare my opinion to that of someone who in some sense ought to agree with me. That is, I would compare my opinion to that of a swinging young professor rather than to the opinion of J. Edgar Hoover or my Aunt Nellie from Nowhere.

The latter people would not provide useful comparisons because I *know* they would disagree with me, and my confidence in my opinion would therefore not be changed.

The swinging young professor (SYP) might or might not agree with me. If he did, I would feel more confident in my opinion. If he did not, I would feel less confident and would feel compelled to do something about it.

I would first try to change SYP's opinion. I would give him literature to read, I would argue with him, and I would get him stoned. If he changed his opinion, my confidence would be increased. It is possible, of course, that during our discussions,

SYP would manage to change my opinion. That would be all right, because I would be more confident in a changed opinion with which SYP agreed than in the original opinion with which SYP did not agree.

It is possible that neither of us would change our opinions. In this case I would cease comparing my opinion to that of SYP and would probably derogate his character and intelligence. If I discovered that we differed in some way that was consistent with our difference of opinion, my tendency to stop comparing my opinion to his would be even stronger. For example, if he didn't believe that alcohol should be legal either, then he wouldn't be the SYP I thought him to be in the first place.

Let us now consider the evaluation of an ability through social comparison. Suppose that you took up tennis and spent several weeks practicing against a backboard. You have never seen anyone else with a tennis racket in his hand, so there is no way to know how good you are. If it is important to find out how good you are, you must find an opponent. Through an unusual set of circumstances, you have three opponents available: the state tennis champion, your five-year-old sister, and a peer who has played against a backboard a little.

Obviously, you would choose to play against your peer. The champion would beat you in straight love sets, and you would do the same to your sister. In neither case would you learn anything at all. You would play your peer, and you would hope to beat him, but not badly. You would hope to beat him because of the unidirectional drive upward which exists for abilities, and you would hope to beat him slightly so that you would have some idea of how good you were. If you beat him badly, you would suspect him of having some physical or psychological infirmity. Your need for evaluation would not be satisfied, because your question is not, How good am I compared to people with infirmities? but, How good am I compared to other healthy people who have had about the same amount of practice I've had?

Let us suppose, however, that you didn't beat him slightly. There are three other alternatives: you beat him badly, he beats you badly, he beats you slightly. If you beat him badly and didn't have anyone else to play with, you would try to change his ability by practicing with him and trying to coach him, hoping that he would become almost as good as you are. On the other hand, if he beat you badly or slightly, you would try to change yourself by practicing long hours against the backboard. If he continued to beat you, it would make a difference how badly he beat you. If the matches were close, you would feel that you were pretty good but not quite as good as you would like to be. If he continued to beat you badly, you wouldn't have any idea how good you were but would ascribe superior status to him: "He's one of those rare naturals on the court." In other words, you would reject him as an appropriate comparison person. The tendency to do this would be even stronger if you discovered that he was a "natural" in other forms of athletics also. His superiority in tennis would be consistent with his overall physical superiority.

At the time SCT was published, there was only one experiment in the literature that provided clear support for the social evaluation of abilities. Let us examine in some detail this experiment by Hoffman, Festinger, and Lawrence (1954).

Two naive subjects and one experimental confederate arrived in the laboratory at approximately the same time and were told that they were to take a three-part intelligence test. The first part of the intelligence test was to be a fairly standard paper and pencil test, the second part was to measure the ability to interact with others, and the third was to be a paper and pencil measure of insight into one's own and others' behavior. For half the subjects the intelligence test was given High Importance. This was done by describing the test as new and extremely valid and by actually composing the test of rather difficult items taken from a variety of intelligence tests. For the other half of the subjects, the test was given Low Importance by saying that it appeared not to really measure anything, but that just a little more evidence was needed in order to be sure of this. The items were easy and a number of them called for value judgments on moralistic questions; thus on the surface the test appeared not to have anything to do with intelligence. According to SCT, the greater the importance of an ability, the greater the pressures to uniformity.

Within each of the Importance conditions, half of the subjects were given what the investigators called a Peer manipulation. This was done by telling the subjects that the three of them had been carefully matched on intelligence and aptitude from existing school records. The remaining subjects in each of the

Importance conditions were given a Non-Peer manipulation. This was done by telling the subjects that one of them was of very superior intelligence and by having the experimental confederate finish the first part of the intelligence test very quickly, long before the naive subjects could do so. Thus the naive subjects could only assume that the experimental confederate was of very superior intelligence.

We have then a total of four conditions: High Importance–Peer, High Importance–Non-Peer, Low Importance–Peer, and Low Importance–Non-Peer.

After completing the first part of the intelligence test (the paper and pencil section which the experimental confederate finished very quickly), subjects were given instructions for the second part of the test. Each subject was given seven triangular pieces of masonite with which to construct squares. Six of the triangles were small and when placed together properly formed a square. The seventh triangle was a large right-angled isosceles triangle. Two of these large triangles placed together made a larger square than the square composed of the six small triangles. The largest square on any one trial won eight points, and these points were to be added to the I.Q. points obtained in the first part of the intelligence test. Any two players on a trial could form a coalition by placing their large triangles together and thereby forming the winning square. If they did this, they had to agree ahead of time on how to divide the eight points between them. Thus, the two subjects could form a coalition on every trial and thereby prevent the confederate from earning any points on this part of the test.

The only exception to these rules was that if an individual formed a square out of his six smaller pieces on the first trial, he automatically won the trial and a bonus of twelve points. On the first trial, the experimental confederate (who had practiced long hours making a square of the six small triangles) immediately put them together and won the regular eight points plus a bonus of twelve, giving him an immediate lead of twenty points over the two naive subjects.

This first trial made it apparent to the naive subjects that they could not hope to beat the experimental confederate by forming individual squares. Thus their only hope of winning any points at all during the second part of the intelligence test was to form a coalition with one another or with the experimental confederate and make a square of two of the large triangular pieces. During the remaining trials the experimental confederate followed a programmed pattern of bargaining, offering first four, then five, then six, then seven of the eight points to one of the naive subjects to form a coalition. If the naive subject refused, the confederate made the same set of offers to the second naive subject. If a subject offered to form a coalition with the confederate, he accepted the offer unless the other naive subject immediately responded with a higher offer.

In this highly contrived but ingenious situation, what would SCT predict? First, subjects in the High Importance conditions should have a greater need to evaluate their ability than subjects in the Low Importance condition; and because self-evaluation is facilitated by similarity to other people, they should work harder to reduce the initial first-trial advantage of the experimental confederate. They could do this by refusing to form coalitions with the confederate and by refusing to offer the confederate an even split of the points when coalitions were formed. As shown in Tables 3 and 4, these results were obtained.

Subjects in the Non-Peer condition should simply cease comparing with the clearly superior experimental confederate and should thus form more coalitions with him and give him more points than subjects in the Peer conditions. Tables 3 and 4 support these predictions.

TABLE 3

Average Points per Coalition for Confederate*

| Task Importance | Status of Confederate | |
	Peer	Non-Peer
High	3.36	3.68
Low	3.68	4.57

Note: Chance = 4.0
*From Hoffman, Festinger, & Lawrence (1954).

An additional result, quite consistent with the theory, was that 63 per cent of the coalitions between the two naive subjects in the Peer conditions resulted in equal splits of the eight points,

TABLE 4

Average Percentage of Coalitions Including Confederate*

| | Status of Confederate | |
Task Importance	Peer	Non-Peer
High	46	55
Low	52	75

Note: Chance = 67.7%
*From Hoffman, Festinger, & Lawrence (1954).

but only 34 per cent of the coalitions in the Non-Peer conditions produced equal divisions of the points. In other words, subjects in the Peer conditions were not competing with one another but were rather trying jointly to reduce the discrepancy between their scores and that of the experimental confederate. Subjects in the Non-Peer conditions, on the other hand, had rejected the confederate as a comparison person, and because of the unidirectional drive upward, were attempting to gain a slight advantage over one another.

I have described this experiment as if it were a lovely confirmation of SCT. In some ways it is, but it also points up a pervasive difficulty with the theory.

In the Low Importance condition, subjects competed with the Peer but rejected the Non-Peer as a comparison person. This is shown by the fact that the Non-Peer entered into a greater-than-chance number of coalitions and received more than an even share per coalition. Subjects in the High Importance condition should have felt stronger pressures toward uniformity than Low Importance subjects. Since pressures toward uniformity lead both to attempts to change others and self and to cessation of comparison with divergent others, *any difference at all* between the two Non-Peer conditions would have supported the theory. Tables 3 and 4 show *greater* competition with the Non-Peer by High Importance subjects than by subjects under Low Importance, and this was taken to indicate attempts to produce similarity between the subject and the confederate. But if High Importance subjects had competed *less* than Low Importance subjects with the Non-Peer, that could have been taken to indicate cessation of comparison.

In more abstract terms, the difficulty with the theory is that a hypothetical construct (pressures toward uniformity) leads to attempts to produce uniformity through competition (or in the case of opinions, through communication) and to rejection of the comparison person as shown by reduced competition and communication. In consequence, the theory, while useful and provocative, is most difficult to confirm or disconfirm.

Some implications of SCT for group formation and societal structure

If the drive for self-evaluation is important in making human beings gregarious, we would expect people to join groups in which the members are similar to themselves in abilities and opinions. We do find a great deal of similarity within groups. Between groups, on the other hand, we find relative dissimilarity. Festinger suggests that ". . . the segmentation into groups is what allows a society to maintain a variety of opinions within it and to accommodate persons with a wide range of abilities" (Festinger, 1954, p. 136).

Segmentation into groups according to levels of ability gives rise to status levels in a society. Even the members of the lower status groups benefit to some extent from segmentation into status levels because, by ignoring other groups and evaluating themselves by comparison with members of their own group, they are able to be relatively satisfied with their ability.

It follows fairly clearly from SCT that the smaller the group, the less secure the self-evaluation. This is because one cannot completely ignore the existence of other groups, and without a sufficient number of members in one's own group, a conflict over the locus of comparison may result. If this is true, one would expect stronger pressures toward uniformity in small groups or minority groups, as a substitute for quantity of membership. This would provide, according to Festinger, an explanation for " . . . the persistent splitting into smaller and smaller factions which is frequently found to occur in minority groups which are under strong pressure from the majority segments of the population" (p. 137).

The full implications of social comparison processes have only begun to be explored. If people evaluate their opinions and abilities through comparison with others, how do they evaluate the appropriateness of their behaviors or what it means behaviorally to have certain personality traits? How do social evaluations affect self-esteem, and how does the desire to protect or enhance self-esteem determine what comparisons are made? In a later chapter we will attempt to answer some of these questions.

Further Developments in
Social Comparison Theory

Affiliation and social comparison

The first major development in SCT after its 1954 publication was a book by Stanley Schachter published in 1959. Schachter's book, *The Psychology of Affiliation,* was actually a description of a number of experiments in which subjects were made anxious, after which their desire to be with other people was measured. Schachter's major point was that " . . . emotions or feelings, like opinions and abilities, require social evaluation when the emotion-producing situation is ambiguous or uninter-pretable in terms of past experience" (p. 129).

The basic experimental procedure was for Dr. Gregor Zil-stein (an evil-sounding pseudonym) to explain to the female sub-jects that were to take part in an experiment on the effects of electric shock. He described the shock as being either extremely painful *(High Anxiety)* or quite mild *(Low Anxiety).* He then noted that there would be a ten-minute delay and that the girls could spend that time either alone or with other girls. Each subject could decide which of the two she herself would do.

Schachter predicted that *High Anxiety* subjects, having a stronger and more ambiguous emotion than *Low Anxiety* sub-jects, would more frequently choose to wait with others, presumably to determine how anxious they *were* and how anxious they *ought* to be. The prediction was confirmed, and Schachter conducted other experiments to determine if the gregarious tendency of the *High Anxiety* subjects was indeed due to evaluative needs.

One implication of SCT is that one can evaluate one's emotions most effectively through comparison with similar others. In order to test this implication, Schachter created two *High Anxiety* conditions. In the *Same State* condition, subjects could wait with other girls who were to take part in the shock experiment. In the *Different State* condition, they could wait with people who were to take part in a different and unrelated experiment. The prediction is clear: subjects should choose to wait with others more frequently when the others are in the *Same State*. The prediction was strongly confirmed. In the *Different State* condition, all of the subjects said they didn't care whether they waited alone or together; in the *Same State* condition, 60 per cent of the subjects chose to wait with others.

Choosing to wait with other people could be prompted by needs for anxiety reduction or by needs for self-evaluation through social comparison, or both. Lawrence Wrightsman (1960), one of Schachter's students, decided to carry the experimental procedure further and actually let subjects wait together or alone. By measuring anxiety before and after the waiting period, Wrightsman wished to determine what effect waiting with others had and, from this, draw conclusions about the needs served.

Wrightsman frightened his subjects by promising a series of injections with a hypodermic needle to raise or lower glucose levels. He said that the injections themselves would be painful, but that the result of the injections would be even worse.

After these instructions, anxiety measures were taken and subjects were assigned to one of two waiting conditions: *Alone* or *Together*. The subjects in each condition waited for five minutes alone or together in groups of four, and another anxiety measure was taken.

Anxiety reduction. There was an overall reduction in anxiety during the five minutes, and the reduction was approximately the same in both conditions. In short, being with others did not have any notable effect in reducing anxiety.

Social evaluation of anxiety. Two manifestations of social comparison processes are: (1) bringing oneself into closer conformity with others, and (2) influencing others to closer agreement with oneself. Both should lead to greater homogeneity of anxiety level. In order to determine whether waiting with others produced more homogeneity than waiting alone, a "homogeneity index" was obtained for each four-person group in the *Together* condition and for statistically-composed groups of four in the *Alone* condition. This index was obtained by dividing the initial range of anxiety ratings within the group (obtained on a 0 to 100 scale) into the post-waiting-period range. An index of less than 1.0 would indicate a smaller range of anxiety levels (greater homogeneity) after the waiting period than before it.

The homogeneity index for the *Alone* condition was .980, indicating that the range of anxiety in the statistically-created groups of four was just slightly less after the waiting period than before it. On the other hand, there was a significant increase in homogeneity in the *Together* condition, the index reaching .831. This is evidence that subjects changed their own anxiety ratings to be more like what they perceived the ratings of the other group members to be, or that they persuaded others to change their feelings of anxiety to be more similar to their own.

Another indication of social comparison processes is the rejection (as a comparison person) of anyone who is extremely dissimilar. In order to test the operation of this principle, Wrightsman divided his groups into three types: those with an initially wide range of anxiety, those with an initially small range of anxiety, and those with an intermediate initial range. Those with a small range should have had their social comparison needs satisfied without further homogenization—others in the group were already similar enough. In those groups with a very large range, the most anxious subjects might be expected to reject as comparison persons the least anxious subjects, and vice versa. If that were the case, one would not expect any increase in homogeneity. Groups with an intermediate range of anxiety initially should, however, move toward much greater homogeneity; the range is great enough to produce forces toward changing self and other, but not so great as to produce rejection of others.

Figure 3 shows quite clearly that these expectations were confirmed. Groups having an intermediate range of anxiety produced much smaller homogeneity indices (moved toward greater homogeneity) than did the other two sets of groups. That this was not due to some statistical artifact is shown by the almost flat line in the *Alone* condition.

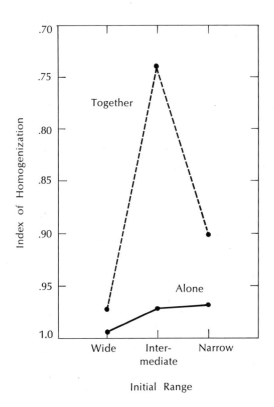

FIGURE 3.   Homogenization of anxiety rating as a function of initial range and waiting conditions (Schachter, 1959).

Taken as a whole, the experiments of Schachter and his students present a reasonably strong case for the argument that individuals compare their own emotional reactions to ambiguous events with the reactions of others. The best evidence for this extension of SCT is the fact that, when made anxious, subjects chose to be with others. Uncertain about the appropriate emotional response, they chose to be with others and observe their responses. Furthermore, in groups in which there was intermediate divergence in initial anxiety ratings, subjects became more homogeneous in the emotional level they reported.

Relating these results to social comparison theory, however, required something of a leap of faith. As Schachter pointed out in the last chapter of his book, "there have, as yet, been no rigorous attempts to demonstrate that unclarity or uncertainty about an opinion or an ability leads to the arousal of affiliative tendencies" (1959, p. 133). What this means is that if one wants to tie emotions, opinions, and abilities together into one theoretical bundle, it would be nice to have identical evidence for each of the three classes.

With this in mind, Roland Radloff (1961) attempted to show that individuals will want to affiliate with others to the extent that they are uncertain about an opinion.

Subjects were asked to indicate what percentage of the cost of college education should be paid by students and their families, as opposed to governmental units. Prior to being asked this question, the subjects were told that the cost of a college education would rise markedly in the next few years and that they, as future parents and taxpayers, should begin to consider what to do about it.

After answering the question about college costs, subjects were placed in one of four conditions: *No Information, Inferior, Peer,* or *Expert.* In the *No Information* condition, subjects were not given any information about opinions of other people; in the *Inferior* condition, they were shown a distribution summarizing the opinions of high school sophomores; in the *Peer* condition, the opinions of college sophomores; and in the *Expert* condition, the opinions of leading economists, university presidents, and state legislators. (In those days, 1959, the opinions of this latter group were valued by students.)

Subjects were then told that discussion groups of college students were being organized at the university to talk about the problem of financing higher education. They were asked to indicate the degree of interest they had in joining such a group.

The SCT prediction is clear: the less reliable information given the subjects, the greater should be the desire to join a discussion group. The prediction was confirmed. The percentage indicating maximum interest in joining a group in each condition was as follows: *No Information,* 40 per cent; *Inferior,* 30 per cent; *Peer,* 19 per cent; *Expert,* 14 per cent.

As with emotion and opinion, there is also evidence that uncertainty about an ability leads to greater affiliative needs. Singer and Shockley (1965) gave subjects an ability test and, subsequently, their scores on the test. Some subjects were given information about the performance of others, while the remaining subjects were not. Subjects were then asked whether they wanted to wait alone or with others while the experimenter prepared to administer an additional test. As we would expect, subjects given information about the performance of others had less desire to wait with others than did the remaining subjects.

There is, then, ample evidence that uncertainty leads to a desire for affiliation; presumably in order to evaluate, through social comparison, the accuracy or appropriateness of one's emotions, abilities, and opinions. There is also evidence that this basic relationship is not quite as simple as all that; people have many needs in addition to comparison needs. A brief illustration may clarify this point.

Schachter spoke of the emotional reaction to impending electric shock as "anxiety." From a psychoanalytic point of view, however, anxiety is a vague feeling of threat or uneasiness which is not attached to any specific event or thing. Thus the emotional reaction of Schachter's subjects might be described more appropriately as "fear." Following this line of reasoning, Irving Sarnoff and Philip Zimbardo (1961) conducted an experiment in which they compared the effects or fear of electric shock with the effects of "oral anxiety." Fear of electric shock was produced in the same way as in Schachter's experiments. Oral anxiety was created by telling subjects they were to suck on some objects commonly associated with infantile oral behavior: baby bottles, rubber nipples, pacifiers, breast shields, and lollipops. Subjects were allowed to wait alone or with others prior to the period of shocking or sucking.

The results were as expected by the investigators. Nearly all the subjects waiting to be shocked chose to wait with others, while half of the subjects waiting to suck the infantile objects chose to wait alone. There are various possible explanations for this result which the reader can list for himself. The important point is that the uncertainty-affiliation relationship has its limits.

Choice of a specific comparison other

A central assumption of SCT is that individuals will choose to compare themselves with someone similar, but the evidence we have examined so far provides only indirect support for the assumption. In recent years, several direct tests have been attempted.

One such test, by John Darley and Eliot Aronson (1966), used Schachter's fear-of-electric-shock paradigm. Each subject was scheduled simultaneously with two confederates. After the experiment had been described, the subject was asked to indicate verbally how nervous or calm she felt (on an eleven-point scale). One confederate indicated that she was one point more nervous than the subject, and the other confederate stated that she was two points less nervous than the subject. The subject was then given the choice of waiting with one of the two confederates (whom she could choose) or alone.

SCT would predict choice of the more nervous confederate, because she was the most similar. But, to the extent that subjects wanted to calm themselves during the waiting period, choice of the less nervous confederate would be appropriate. The SCT prediction was confirmed: subjects chose to wait with the more nervous *but more similar* confederate.

An additional condition run by Darley and Aronson points up another spike of complexity, however. In a *High Uncertainty* condition, subjects were told that " . . . this is one of the first groups we have run. So we just don't have data on the pain caused by the electric shocks . . ." In contrast, subjects in the *High Fear* condition had been told that the shocks would be quite painful.

High Fear subjects were quite nervous; they knew they had reason to be nervous, and they chose to wait with the most similar other available in order to determine if it were appropriate to be that nervous. *High Uncertainty* subjects were only slightly nervous and they weren't sure they had any reason to be nervous at all. For these subjects, the desire to eliminate nervousness altogether overcame their need for a similar comparison person, and they chose to wait with the less nervous confederate or alone.

This is complicated. The argument we have been pursuing is that uncertainty about the appropriateness of certain emotional responses leads to choice of a comparison person feeling a similar level of emotional response. But then we encounter an experimental condition called "High Uncertainty" and find that subjects chose to wait alone or with a dissimilar other. The difficulty lies in the meaning of "uncertainty." High Fear subjects felt a clear emotion and were uncertain if it was at the appropriate level. High Uncertainty subjects, on the other hand, did not know what emotion, if any, that they should experience. Believing as most of us do that health is better than sickness, and wealth better than poverty, they acted in such a way as to achieve serenity rather than nervousness.

Other experimental attempts to delineate what kinds of people are chosen for comparison have also extended SCT into the area of personality traits. If humans frequently evaluate their opinions, abilities, and emotions through comparison with others, it seems reasonable that they also evaluate their personality predispositions in the same way. Personality traits are rather like abilities in that they are relatively enduring. However, it is nearly always desirable to have as much as possible of an ability, while many personality traits are definitely undesirable.

This latter fact furnishes interesting research possibilities. According to SCT, we should choose to compare ourselves with someone having slightly more ability than we ourselves do (at least in the competitive Western culture). This might imply, with regard to the evaluation of personality traits, that comparison should usually be with someone slightly better off than we are. If the trait is one we value, comparison should be with someone having slightly more of it; if the trait is a negative one, comparison should be with someone having slightly less of it.

This implication was tested in an experiment by Wheeler, Shaver, Jones, Goethals, Cooper, Robinson, Gruder, and Butzine (1969). Groups of nine subjects each were given a fictitious paper-and-pencil test. Subjects in the Flexibility condition were told that the test measured intellectual flexibility, which was described as being a very desirable trait to have. Subjects in a Rigidity condition were told that the test measured the undesirable trait, Intellectual Rigidity.

The experimenter explained that, in order to protect the identity of the subjects, he would assign each of them an identification letter, A through I. Actually, he assigned each subject the same identification letter, H. When the tests had been completed, the experimenter quickly scored them and, using the identification letters, wrote the rank order of scores on the blackboard. The rank order indicated that subject H (each of the subjects believed himself to be H) had obtained the middle score in the group. Each subject was then told privately what his own numerical score was. The approximate numerical scores of the highest and the lowest members of the rank order were written on the blackboard also. At this point, each subject had the information shown in Table 5.

TABLE 5

Information Available to Subject Prior to Comparison Choice*

Rank Order	Score
G	550-600
I	
D	
A	
H = Subject	310
F	
C	
E	
B	25-75

*From Wheeler, et al. (1969).

The experimenter then said the following:

I would like to give you some information about the scores of the other members in the group. For reasons that I can't go into right now but will later, I can't show you everybody's score, but I would like to give you the score of one other person in the group. This will give you some relevant information. So, on the card in front of you, please write the identification letter of the person whose score you would most like to see (Wheeler et al., 1969, p. 223).

The SCT prediction for the *Flexible* condition is that sub-jects should choose to see the score of the person directly above them in the rank order, a person highly similar but somewhat better off. This was indeed the predominant choice, accounting for 47 per cent of all subjects. In the *Rigidity* condition, the pre-diction was again confirmed, with the predominant choice being the person directly below the subject in the rank order (44 per cent). This person was, of course, highly similar but somewhat better off.

Overall, every single subject in the *Flexible* condition chose to see the score of someone better off than himself, and nearly every subject (87 per cent) in the *Rigidity* condition did so.

The data, then, are clear—but what is the explanation? Does hope spring so eternal in the human subject's breast that he be-lieves he will find that he is *almost* as good as his "betters"? For the moment we can only speculate that this is the case. But there is another question. Do we not, as humans, sometimes compare ourselves with those who are clearly inferior to us on some dimension so that we may feel superior? There is an old Indian saying, in the movies at least, that "even a hawk is an eagle among crows." In order to test this possibility, Karl Hakmiller (1966) performed an experiment similar in format to the one just described.

Hakmiller's subjects were tested in groups of six. All subjects had taken the Minnesota Multiphasic Personality Inventory (MMPI) at the time they entered the university. They were told that from this paper-and-pencil test it was possible to predict with about 50 per cent accuracy the rank order of the group members on the degree of hostility they felt toward their parents. It was further explained that it was necessary to compare the hostility measured by the MMPI with the hostility measured by a much more precise physiological measure, which consisted of galvanic skin responses to projective slides.

The hostility measure was taken, and subjects were told that the trait which had been measured was "hostility toward one's own parents." This trait was described to subjects in a *High Threat* condition as quite terrible, leading eventually to a deteri-oration of the personality. To subjects in a *Low Threat* condition, the trait was described as being a desirable one despite its neg-ative sound.

After giving the appropriate description of "hostility toward one's own parents," the experimenter wrote the rank order of the six subjects on the blackboard. This rank order was of the hostility scores obtained from the MMPI. It was thus a prediction of the rank order that should have been obtained from the more accurate physiological measure. Unknown to the subjects, each of them had been given the same identification letter, D. The rank order showed person D to be fifth from the top in the group of six. The subject was thus led to expect a low hostility score as measured by the galvanic skin response.

Hakmiller's strategy was to threaten subjects by presenting them with unexpectedly high hostility scores. He reasoned that this might cause them to engage in defensive comparison—to compare themselves with someone much worse off (more hostile) in order to reduce the threat to themselves.

An unexpectedly unfavorable score was given to subjects by privately informing each one that her score, as measured physiologically, was either 60 or 80. The subject had been told that the range of the scale was 0 to 100 and that, according to the MMPI, she had the next to lowest score in the group. This should have led the subject to expect her score from the physiological measurement to be relatively low, perhaps 30 to 40. Finding, however, that her score was actually 60 or 80 was surprising and, particularly to the *High Threat* subjects, threatening.

After the subjects had been given their scores, each was asked to indicate privately to the experimenter which one score in the group he would like to see.

The prediction was that *High Threat* subjects should have a greater tendency than *Low Threat* subjects to choose to see the score of someone predicted to be much worse off than themselves, i.e., having a higher score. The prediction was nicely confirmed in that 54 per cent of the *High Threat* subjects chose the highest score in the group, compared to only 22 per cent of the *Low Threat* subjects. Very few subjects in either condition chose to see the score of the one person in the group who was predicted to have less hostility than themselves.

It was also expected that subjects who had been given a score of 80 would be more threatened than those given a score of 60 and would have a greater tendency to choose to see a high score. Surprisingly, there was no difference at all between the two groups. Perhaps 60 was so unexpectedly high that any higher score could have no additional psychological impact.

While there may be other ways to explain the results of this experiment, the defensive comparison explanation is certainly an attractive one. Surely we do at times engage in defensive comparison, and Hakmiller has tried to specify the condition under which we do: When unexpectedly negative information is obtained about the self, defensive comparison may occur.

Social Facilitation Revisited

In 1965 Robert Zajonc (pronounced "Zyons") reviewed the massive literature on social facilitation, which was described briefly in Chapter 1. Zajonc developed an elegantly simple theoretical formulation which he believed would account for the various results from experiments on social facilitation.

Zajonc first postulated that the presence of other people is physiologically arousing. He likened this physiological arousal to a generalized drive known in Hullian learning theory as "D". In the learning theory, D (Drive) $\times H$ (Habit) $= B$ (Behavior).

One simple derivation from the simple formula, $D \times H = B$, is that as drive increases, the stronger habits increase in strength at a faster rate than the weaker habits. An example should clarify why this is so. Suppose an individual has two habits with regard to food. The first habit is to go to a nearby restaurant, and this habit has a strength of 10. The second habit is to rummage through the refrigerator and find something to eat, and this habit has the strength of 9. If we assume drive in each case to have the strength of 1, then the behavior potential for going to the restaurant is 10 ($1 \times 10 = 10$) and the behavior potential for going through the refrigerator is 9 ($1 \times 9 = 9$). There is a difference between the two acts of 1 unit in behavioral potential. If we now increase ten-fold the strength of drive, giving it the value of 10, the behavioral potential for going to the restaurant is 100 ($10 \times 10 = 100$), while the behavioral potential for going through the refrigerator is 90. There is now a difference of 10 units in the behavioral potential of the two acts. Thus, by increasing drive we have increased the probability that the originally dominant response will be performed.

If the presence of others does increase drive or arousal, and if drive does increase the probability that dominant responses will be performed, then well-learned tasks should be performed better in the presence of other people, because the correct responses are dominant. On difficult or poorly learned tasks, however, it is likely that incorrect responses are dominant, and the presence of other people should lead to poor performance. This reasoning fits well with the results of the experiments mentioned in Chapter 1. Allport found that on several tests—chain word association, vowel cancellation, reversible perspective, multiplication—individuals performed better in groups than when alone. These are very easy tasks, in which the correct response is dominant. On the other hand, individuals performed worse in groups than when alone in a problem-solving test in which they were to disprove arguments of ancient philosophers. Presumably, this is not a well-learned task, and incorrect responses were dominant.

Zajonc believed that his argument applied not only to humans, but also to rats, ants, and cockroaches. One study cited as evidence showed that pairs of ants started nest building much faster than solitary ants in the same artificial environment. Zajonc himself has reported an experiment in which cockroaches were required to escape from a bright floodlight into a dark goal box. If the escape route was a straight runway, the roaches in pairs did better than roaches tested alone. If, however, the roaches had to choose a certain turn in a maze in order to reach the goal box, animals in pairs did poorer than animals tested alone. This supports Zajonc's formulation if we accept the quite reasonable assumption that moving straight away from a light is a dominant response for a cockroach and that learning to turn at right angles to a light in a maze is a very subordinant response.

Zajonc's position is a very attractive one indeed. It is an extremely simple formulation—that mere presence of other organisms increases arousal and thereby increases the probability that the dominant response will be emitted—that is applicable to organisms from humans to at least ants and cockroaches.

Many examples of such a thing operating on humans come easily to mind. Among professional and top amateur athletes, for example, it is certain that the dominant response is the correct athletic response, and these people perform much better in a public game than in a private practice. They also talk about being "up" (physiologically aroused) for a game. The same is true of professional entertainers, who sometimes complain that the audience was too small to bring forth their best efforts.

Most of us have had the experience of being tired and sluggish and feeling sorry for ourselves, only to have friends drop by, at which time we feel more aroused and more our usual optimistic selves.

The television industry must agree with Zajonc, because they seldom show a comedy without a cued, live studio audience or a soundtrack of a laughing crowd. They want to arouse us by making us think we are part of a group. (One only wonders why they think laughing at their shows would be a dominant response for anyone.) There are some funny movies, however, and most of us would admit that we would laugh more in a theater where others are laughing than when watching the same movies alone at home.

Zajonc advised students to lock themselves into their rooms and study alone so that other people would not increase the probability of responding incorrectly. Assuming that the material was learned, exams should then be taken on a stage in front of a large audience. The student whose dominant response is to sleep rather than study should not heed Zajonc's advice.

The difficulty with Zajonc's position is that people are never "merely present." People are always either ignoring you or watching you or modeling for you or imitating you, or in some way, from your point of view, more than "merely present." An experiment by Thomas Henchy and David Glass (1969) highlights this difficulty.

Subjects were high school and college males who believed the experiment to be concerned with physiological processes involved in word recognition. Physiological apparatus was attached to the subject and he was then shown a number of nonsense words projected on a screen. Each time a word was shown, the subject pronounced it aloud. There were ten core words. During the training procedure two of these words were presented once each, another two were presented twice each, another two were presented four times each, another two were presented eight times each, and a final two were presented sixteen times each. The purpose of this procedure was to make the verbalizing or pronouncing of some of the words quite dominant over the other words. After training, the subject was instructed that the foreign words he had just learned to pronounce would be presented on the screen at speeds and illuminations which would make recognition on most trials extremely difficult. However, the subject's task was to say what word was shown on each presentation, even if he had to guess.

On many of the trials one of the original core words used in training was presented. But on what the investigators called the "pseudo-recognition trials," new nonsense words of the same length and structure were presented. Since the subject expected only one of the original core words to be presented, he had to choose one of these words on the pseudo-recognition trials. We would expect a general tendency for the subject to most frequently choose those core words which were presented most frequently in training; that is, we would expect subjects generally to make the dominant response. The point of the experiment was to determine in which of four experimental conditions choice of the dominant response would be most likely.

In the *Alone* condition, subjects were led to believe that not even the experimenter would be aware of whether they correctly perceived the words or not. In the *Expert Together* condition, two confederates were introduced as experts in perception and human learning, and the confederates sat in the room with the subject during the test trials. In a *Non-expert Together* condition, the same two confederates were presented as students who simply wanted to observe a psychological experiment; they stayed in the room with the subject during the test trials. In the *Alone Recorded* condition, subjects were led to believe that their performance on the recognition task was being tape-recorded and filmed for later evaluation by specialists in perception and human learning.

Henchy and Glass did not believe that the mere presence of others increases the probability that the dominant response will be emitted. Rather, they believed that when one is apprehensive about being evaluated, the probability of the dominant response is increased. Thus, they predicted that the dominant responses would be given more frequently in the *Expert Together* and *Alone Recorded* conditions than in the *Non-expert Together* and *Alone* conditions. There should have been no apprehension about being evaluated in the *Alone* condition and very little in the *Non-expert Together* condition. In the *Alone Recorded* condition there should have been more evaluative apprehension, and the *Expert Together* condition should have created the greatest amount of apprehension. The results strongly confirmed the predictions. The dominant response was, of course, the verbalization on the pseudo-recognition trials of the two core words which had been presented sixteen times in the training session. Use of these words was most common in the *Expert Together* condition, then in the *Alone Recorded* condition, then in the *Non-expert Together* condition, and least of all in the *Alone* condition. Physiological measures of arousal—heart rate and skin conductance—also failed to support Zajonc's prediction that the presence of other people would produce greater arousal. Nor did evaluative apprehension produce greater levels of arousal.

It should be very clearly noted that this experiment does not destroy the value of the Zajonc position. It merely suggests a modification. Rather than saying that the *mere presence* of other people increases the probability that the dominant response will be emitted, we must say that the presence, actual or implied, of other people who create *evaluative apprehension* increases the probability of the dominant response. Given this modification, Zajonc's position is a very significant contribution to a greater understanding of social facilitation effects.

Behavioral and Hysterical Contagion

Long before scientific method was applied to social behavior, the concept of "contagion" was a part of social psychology. Sociological writers used the concept to explain mass behavior such as riots, panics, and mobs—situations in which some mood or behavior spreads quickly and spontaneously through a group. Earlier writers believed that crowds were feminine (that is, hysterical), that they were therefore subject to the dissociation of the hypnotized, and that they were uncritically receptive of any dramatically expressed emotion or behavior.

Despite the long history of the concept, empirical interest in contagion did not appear until 1950, the major reason being that riots and panics in large groups are not very susceptible to empirical study. With the advent of group therapy during World War II, however, it became apparent that contagion occurred in small groups, and in 1949 Fritz Redl, a psychiatrist trained in Vienna, wrote that "with the development of Group Therapy . . . the phenomenon of contagion deserves . . . the foreground of our practical as well as theoretical interests" (Redl, 1949, p. 316).

Redl's concern was to specify those conditions under which contagion occurs and those under which it does not. He believed that it occurs when the imitator has an impulse to express himself in certain ways but has ego or superego controls just strong enough to prevent open expression. For example, the individuals in a therapy group might feel very angry toward the therapist and might be barely able to restrain their expression of the anger. If one group member, called by Redl the "initiator," openly and without any indication of fear or guilt expresses hostility toward the group leader, and if some or all of the other group members begin to express hostility toward the leader, contagion has occurred. According to Redl, the following occurs psychologically in the imitators: "the sudden visualization of fearless and guiltless enjoyment of what they really wanted to do sways their own labile balance between desire and control in favor of the former" (p. 321). Wheeler (1966) extended Redl's theoretical position. In effect, behavioral contagion was defined by the following four sets of conditions: (1) an observer is motivated to behave in a certain way; (2) the observer knows how to perform the behavior in question, but is not performing it; (3) the observer sees a model perform the behavior; and (4) the observer, after observing the model, performs the behavior. The assumption is that when these four events occur the model has performed the function of reducing the observer's internal restraints against performing the behavior.

An observer has internal restraints against performing a behavior either because he in some way fears the practical consequences of performing it or because he considers it in some way immoral or dishonorable. When a model performs a behavior he is in essence stating that he considers the behavior to be justified morally and that he assesses the situation as being safe in a practical sense. Moreover, if no negative consequences accrue to the model for his behavior, he has demonstrated the safety of the situation.

One may think of the observer as being in an approach-avoidance conflict, in which the avoidance tendencies are somewhat greater than the approach tendencies. The model, by reducing the strength of the avoidance tendencies, removes or lessens the observer's conflict. Conceptually, this is quite different from the Asch situation or from the type of influence situation studied by Festinger and his colleagues. In those situations the subject has an opinion or perception and is in no conflict at all about this until he discovers that other people have different opinions or perceptions. When he discovers this, he must in some way resolve the conflict by himself. Thus, in contagion, other people (the model) reduce or resolve the conflict for the observer, while in the conformity and social pressures experiments other people create the conflict and leave the individual doing the breast-stroke in a sea of doubt.

In this discussion of contagion the response has been spoken of as if it were an all-or-none event; it occurs or it does not occur. This is not a necessary consequence of the formulation and perhaps one should think of the observer as being in a quasi-stationary equilibrium, with driving forces and restraining forces maintaining behavior at a given level. When the model reduces the strength of the restraining forces, the individual may increase the frequency or intensity of responding.

An interesting example of the difference between contagion and what is normally called conformity may be seen in the effect of the non-unanimous majority in the Asch situation. Prior to the appearance of a partner who gives the correct judgment, the subject is instigated to give the correct judgment but experiences internal restraints against doing so—because the unanimous majority up to that point has given a different judgment. Approximately a third of the time the subject resolves this conflict created by the majority by giving the incorrect judgment; the socially created restraints against giving the correct judgment are too great. But if one member of the group is instructed to give the correct judgment, the subject ceases to conform to majority opinion. The partner has reduced the subject's restraints against verbalizing what he perceives.

After reviewing a number of experiments, Wheeler (1966) proposed five summary statements of a theoretical nature:

1. ". . . depending upon the initial strength of the approach and avoidance gradients, the observer's behavior may or may not be an exact imitation of the model's behavior" (p. 185). Suppose that an observer and a model are listening to their host at a cocktail party tell a long story. The observer wants to go to the bathroom but hates to be rude. The model, being more of an individualist or less of a gentleman, leaves during the story to mix himself another drink. This reduces the observer's restraints and he leaves for the bathroom.

2. "... the probability of the occurrence of behavioral contagion is greatest when the avoidance gradient is just slightly higher than the approach gradient" (p. 186). If restraints are too great, observation of a model will not reduce them enough to change behavior; if restraints are too weak, the observer will express his impulse regardless of what the model does.

3. "... the observer vicariously performs the behavior performed by the model, and the observer vicariously experiences the consequences of the behavior which are overtly experienced by the model. To the extent then that the model is rewarded or not punished, the observer's avoidance gradient is lowered" (p. 187).

4. "... to the extent that the model appears to be or is known to be generally rewarded or not punished for whatever behavior he emits, the observer's avoidance gradient is lowered for whatever behavior the model performs" (p. 187).

5. "... after the occurrence of contagion in a situation in which the observer is not punished for his behavior, the observer will like the model more than previously and will feel more similar to him on a variety of dimensions ..." (p. 190).

Wheeler further suggested that there are three kinds of restraints: (1) group-derived restraints (we never flirt in my group), (2) ego or superego restraints (it is wrong to flirt), and (3) authoritarian restraints (if I flirt with her, he will hit me).

The most effective model for reducing group-derived restraints should be a central and high status group member. Contagion should spread rapidly, because every member who performs the behavior reduces the restraints still further. Ego or superego restraints should best be reduced by someone whose control and moral judgment we respect, and who shows no hesitation or guilt about his behavior. Authoritarian restraints will be reduced by anyone who performs the behavior in the presence of the punitive authority and gets away with it.

The type of research generated by this theoretical position will be illustrated with an experiment by Wheeler and Smith (1967). The research was an attempt to determine (a) whether verbal censure of an aggressive model would affect subsequent aggression by an observer, and (b) whether there would be a differential effect of censure delivered by the experimenter, a peer, or the aggressive model himself. Measures of liking for the model were also obtained to test the hypothesis that a model who reduces restraints will be liked.

To describe the experiment in detail would take more space than is available; consequently, I will give a very brief overview and ask the reader to be trusting.

Each subject engaged in a discussion with three confederates. One of the confederates, whom we will refer to as the Target, expressed opinions designed to anger the subject, a young naval recruit. One of the other confederates, whom we will refer to as the Model, aggressed verbally against the Target in four of the five conditions; in the fifth condition, labeled the No Model condition, the Model disagreed with the Target but did not aggress against him.

The four conditions in which the Model aggressed against the Target differed with regard to verbal censure of the Model for his aggression. In the No Censure condition, no one said anything to the Model about his aggression. In the E Censure condition, the experimenter interrupted the conversation immediately after the Model's aggression and censured him with the statement, "It's no good flying off the handle like that." In the Peer Censure condition, the third confederate censured the Model with the same words. And in the Self-Censure condition, the Model paused for a moment after having aggressed and censured himself.

After all of this occurred, the subject had an opportunity to express aggression toward the Target. He did this by choosing from a scaled list of expressions of hostility the phrase that best described his feelings toward the Target; he then elaborated on why he felt this way. At the end of the discussion, the subject indicated privately on a questionnaire how much he liked each of the other participants.

The results for both aggression toward the Target and liking for the Model are presented in Figure 4.

According to contagion theory, there should have been more aggression in the No Censure condition than in any other, and there should have been a large difference between the No Censure and No Model conditions, as restraints were not reduced in this latter condition. It is apparent from Figure 4 that both predictions were confirmed.

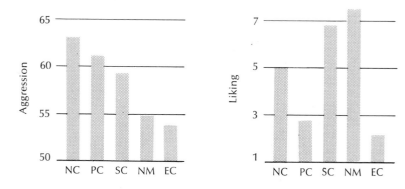

FIGURE 4.   Aggression toward the Target and liking for the Model
by experimental conditions (Wheeler and Smith, 1967).

The theory makes no clear predictions about which type of censure should have been most effective in reinstating restraints against aggression. In fact, *E Censure* was extremely effective, while *Peer Censure* and *Self-Censure* were only slightly so. It should be noted that the experimenter was a naval commander, and the young recruits were probably terrified of him.

Let us turn to the part of Figure 4 dealing with liking for the Model. According to the theory, liking for the Model should be greatest in those conditions in which he most effectively reduced restraints against aggression. The prediction was clearly disconfirmed. In fact, the Model was most liked when he did not aggress at all *(No Model* condition).

The most interesting result was that the Model was least liked in those conditions in which someone else censured him, either the Experimenter or the Peer. Apparently the subject adopted as his own the negative attitudes expressed by these others. This created a particularly surprising effect in the *Peer Censure* condition: the subject imitated the Model's aggression but disliked him nevertheless.

Hysterical contagion

In a textile factory in a small southern city, in the early sixties, a strange epidemic broke out. Over a period of several weeks, more than a fourth of the 200 female employees were bitten by a mysterious bug. The illness was characterized by nervousness, nausea, weakness, and numbness, while the actual bites were very similar to gnat bites. The situation attracted national publicity, but the experts that were called in to search the plant for the offending bug could find only black ants, houseflies, gnats, beetles, and chiggers, none of which could have caused the extreme reaction seen in the employees. The situation also attracted the attention of two Duke University sociologists, Alan Kerckhoff and Kurt Back (1968). These men saw in the situation an opportunity to study what they termed "hysterical contagion"—the dissemination of a set of symptoms among a population in a situation in which no manifest basis for the symptoms can be established.

The investigators believed that tension or "strain" would have to play an important part in causing the mysterious illness. This belief was somewhat confirmed by the fact that the epidemic occurred at the height of the production season, when the female employees were working a great deal of overtime. A four-point index of strain was devised so that each woman could be characterized according to the amount of strain she was experiencing at the time.

The first part of the index was how much overtime the woman was working. The second part of the index was whether the woman was providing half or more of the family income. Thirdly, failing to mention the supervisor as a person to go to with a complaint was counted as a source of strain, because it indicated a lack of belief in the plant organization. Finally, seeing a great deal of variation in work output among the members of one's work section indicated strain because of the implication that some people worked harder than others.

Using these criteria, each woman achieved a strain score from 0 to 4, and the investigators confirmed their hunch that the higher the strain score, the more likely a woman was to be bitten by the mysterious bug.

The friendship patterns in the group were also examined. It was found that if a woman was not an intimate friend of anyone affected, she was not likely to be affected either, unless of course she had a very high strain index. On the other hand, if a woman counted as intimate friends two or more of the women who were bitten by the bug, she was very likely to be affected. In other words, having a friend bitten by the bug apparently increased one's belief that indeed the bug existed.

The investigators found that in the initial stages of the epidemic, social isolates—those who had few close friends in the plant and were not well liked—were most likely to be bitten. Toward the end of the epidemic, when large numbers of women had been affected, friendship patterns appeared to be of little importance. But during the major portion of the epidemic, when the symptoms were spreading most rapidly, friendship patterns were extremely important.

The early victims, the social isolates, had a history of nervousness and fainting. They were highly dissatisfied with their jobs and their role as workers. Not having any close social ties in the factory, they were free from any group standards which might have prevented their bizarre behavior.

Another interesting demonstration of the importance of social influence is described as follows:

> If a woman were the first of a network of close associates to become stricken, she was more likely to faint, whereas later cases in the network reported to the doctor before fainting. Evidently, the experience of the first case in the network was enough to convince the women that the threat was really serious and that medical aid was necessary (Kerckhoff and Back, 1968, p. 171).

In a theoretical treatment of the results, the authors distinguished between behavioral contagion and hysterical contagion. Their view of behavioral contagion was essentially the same as that of Wheeler, described previously. Individual members of a group have strong personal needs and pre-existing restraints against performing the behavior that would satisfy the needs. Knowledge that a group member has performed the behavior reduces the restraints for other group members.

In hysterical contagion, as in behavioral contagion, there are also strong personal needs. In the case of the mysterious bug, the need was to stop working in the dressmaking section of the textile factory. The need was to have more time at home, to have more time with the children, to escape from the poorly organized factory in which workers contributed unequally to the output. And hysterical contagion shares with behavioral contagion the existence of strong restraints against doing what is desired. Many of the women were providing half the family income, and they simply could not afford to cut down on the number of hours worked. Furthermore, they could not admit to themselves that the job was too much for them while their friends continued to work at it.

In short, in both behavioral contagion and hysterical contagion there are strong needs to perform an act and there are strong restraints against performing that act.

At this point the two types of contagion diverge. In behavioral contagion the model performs the act the observer wants to perform and thereby reduces the observer's restraints against performing the act. The observer then performs the act, and the tension or strain is reduced. Hysterical contagion, on the other hand, appears to be due to a failure to overcome the restraints preventing the expression of the impulse. The observer sees the model scream that she has been bitten by a bug, and then faint. This is not the kind of behavior that the observer wants to perform; in fact, the model's behavior merely increases the strain of being in the factory and the desire to leave. In addition to the previous sources of strain, there is now the very real possibility that there are dangerous bugs about, possibly carried in with shipments of textiles from South America.

An almost universal human reaction to high levels of strain and tension is the development of physiological symptoms—headaches, nervousness, nausea, etc. The presence of the bug in the factory increased the symptoms and at the same time provided a possible explanation for them. With each succeeding person who was bitten by the bug, it became easier to believe that one's physiological symptoms were due to bug bites, particularly if one of these persons was a liked and trusted friend. And particularly if one's tension level and physiological symptoms were high to begin with.

In short, hysterical contagion is characterized by (1) a shared sense of tension, (2) a physiological expression of tension in a set of symptoms, (3) the definition of these symptoms as being from some external source, and (4) the dissemination and growth of the tension and the acceptance of this definition in the group.

In behavioral contagion the model performs the act or

expresses the impulse that the observer wants to perform or express. In hysterical contagion the model performs an act which the observer does not want to perform, which merely increases the observer's tension and simultaneously creates a belief in another negative element (the bug) in the environment.

13

Some Conditions of Obedience and Disobedience to Authority

Place yourself in the following situation:

You arrive at a psychological laboratory to take part in an experiment on learning. You are immediately paid the $4.50 you have been promised for taking part in the experiment. You find that another subject is to take part in the experiment with you and that he has already arrived. The experimenter explains that one of you will be the "teacher" and one the "learner" in a study of the effects of negative reinforcement on the learning of word pairs. The negative reinforcement will be shock.

The experimenter flips a coin and thereby designates you as the "teacher." The learner, a fifty-year-old man, is strapped into a chair, and an electrode is attached to his wrist. The experimenter explains that you will read the first word of a series of word pairs and that the learner will try to respond with the correct second word. Whenever he makes a mistake, you will be required to administer the negative reinforcement.

You are taken into the next room and seated before a shock generator which has a row of thirty switches ranging from 15 volts to 450 volts. You are told to start at the lowest level of shock on the first mistake and to increase the shock by one switch (15 volts) for each subsequent mistake.

The learner makes so many mistakes that you progress rapidly to higher shock levels. At 75 volts, the learner grunts; at 100 volts, he complains; at 150 volts, he demands to be released. He complains and yells as you increase the shock until at 285 volts he gives an agonizing scream and shouts that he can no longer give answers. Following the instructions of the experimenter, you continue reading the words and treating the learner's lack of response as an error, increasing the shock each time until you reach 450 volts, labeled "Danger—Severe Shock." The learner continues to scream in agony with each shock.

If you hesitate to continue with the shock, the experimenter says "Please continue," then "The experiment requires that you continue," then "It is absolutely essential that you go on," and finally "You have no choice but to go on."

Would you continue through the last shock? How many people do you know who would go to 450 volts?

Subjects were male adults from the New Haven, Connecticut area, ranging from 20 to 50 years of age and drawn from all occupational levels.

An astonishing 62 per cent of these men obeyed the experimenter completely! Forty psychiatrists from a leading medical school had predicted that only one-tenth of one per cent would do so.

This experiment, and many variations on it, was performed by Stanley Milgram. Milgram was concerned that the atrocities committed against the Jews in World War II could not be explained by the simple assertion that obedience to authority is the basic characterological flaw of the German people. He believed, rather, that even United States citizens would be much more obedient to authority than anyone would expect. Even Milgram was surprised, however, that so many subjects completed the entire series of shocks.

When I first heard of this research, I dismissed it as unbelievable and assumed that the subjects had somehow known that they weren't really shocking anyone. But having now seen auxiliary data and films of experimental sessions, I must accept the data as being perfectly valid.

One explanation for the results might be that subjects knew that an institution of Yale's stature would not allow anyone to be harmed in research. To answer this objection, Milgram ran additional subjects in a sparsely furnished office suite in a run-down building in Bridgeport. The study was not connected to Yale in any way but was conducted by a fictitious Research Associates of Bridgeport. The number of obedient subjects decreased slightly but not significantly.

In one variation of the experiment, the learner was placed in the same room with the teacher, about a foot and a half in front of him. Thus the subject had to look at the writhing pain (of the professional actor) as well as listen to the screams. In this condition, 40 per cent of the subjects still were fully obedient.

In a further attempt to reduce obedience, Milgram ran another variation in which the subject had to press the learner's hand against a shockplate and hold it there while pressing the shock switch. Thirty per cent of the subjects went all the way through the shock series.

With the subject and the learner in separate rooms, the physical presence of the experimenter was varied. Rather than sitting close to the subject and giving him commands, the experimenter gave them by telephone. Only 22 per cent of the subjects were fully obedient in this condition. A number of the subjects pretended to be obedient, however. While giving only the lowest level of shock, they assured the experimenter that they were indeed increasing the shock on each trial.

In another variation, the subject was one of three "teachers." The first teacher, an experimental confederate, read the words. The second teacher, also a confederate, told the learner whether he was right or wrong. The subject's duty was to deliver the shock. At 150 volts, Teacher 1 said he would not continue, and he resisted the commands of the experimenter to do so. Teacher 2 and the subject were instructed to continue with the task. At 210 volts, Teacher 2 said that he would not continue to take part. At this point the subject had two models for disobedience, but was commanded by the experimenter to continue the experiment alone. Only 10 per cent of the subjects obeyed him. This situation fits very nicely the definition of behavioral contagion given in the last chapter; the two models reduced the subject's restraints against doing what he wanted to do. Of course, if the experimenter had immediately shot both defiant models, restraints would have remained high. Interestingly enough, very few of the defiant subjects admitted that they had been influenced at all by the confederates. We know that they were influenced, of course, by comparing their behavior to that of subjects in other conditions.

All these experimental variations make it quite clear that the tendency to obey an authority figure, who orders destructive actions, is strong. The subjects were in a conflict between the fear of disobeying an authority and the concern with inflicting intense pain on another human being. The conflict was evidenced by the subjects' sweating, groaning, trembling, stuttering, and biting their lips while continuing to administer the shock. Nearly half of the subjects engaged in nervous laughter and smiling. About 10 per cent of them had uncontrollable long seizures of nervous laughter.

Why, then, did subjects continue to obey? Milgram has suggested that the subject enters an altered state of thinking when confronted with commands from an authority figure. The altered state allows the subject to cope with the strain caused by the conflict. This state is characterized by (1) a concentration on the narrow technical performance of the task, ignoring the meaning of saying the words and pulling the switches; (2) a belief that the experimenter rather than he is responsible for his actions; and (3) a feeling of "counter-anthropomorphism" about the experiment. The latter is a tendency to think of an experiment designed and conducted by a human as something impersonal and inexorable.

Milgram believed that his subjects were kept in this altered state by a set of "binding factors," such as their politeness, their desire to uphold their initial promise, and their dread of interpersonal confrontation.

The tendency to deny personal responsibility was pronounced. In an experimental variation similar to the one already described, there were three "teachers," and the subject's job was to pull a master switch just before one of the confederates pressed the switch that delivered the shock. Over 90 per cent of the subjects were fully obedient, justifying their behavior by the fact that they weren't actually shocking anyone. One can better understand the destruction of European Jewry. As Milgram has pointed out, Eichmann didn't kill anyone, and the men dropping the gas pellets were just doing what they had to do.

A final note. These experiments have been criticized on ethical grounds, some critics feeling that the self-knowledge gained by the subjects might be psychologically damaging. Milgram took careful precautions against this, however. The debriefing involved a lengthy discussion with the experimenter and a friendly reconciliation with the victim. A psychiatrist was unable to find any traces of damage in a sample of the subjects. Less than 2 per cent of the subjects said they wished they had not taken part in the experiment, and 84 per cent were glad to have done so. Three out of four subjects said they had learned something of personal importance, and many of them asked to be used in further research.

14

Intervention into Emergencies

Kitty Genovese was stabbed to death in 1964 in a residential area of New York City. The murderer took about thirty minutes to kill her, stabbing her, running away, and then returning to stab her again. Miss Genovese screamed and cried for help during most of this time. The incident gained national publicity because thirty-eight people watched the entire murder from the safety of their apartments, and not one of them even called the police.

The mass media talked about apathy, anomie, urban alienation, and the dehumanizing effect of big-city living. Two young New York City social psychologists, Bibb Latané and John Darley, did not feel that such explanations really explained anything. They began to think about the thirty-eight people in a different way. The media were saying, in effect, "It is terrible that so many people watched the murder without any one of them trying to help." Latané and Darley began to think, "Perhaps no one helped *because* there were so many people watching."

It was clearly someone's responsibility to call the police. Each individual, however, aware that the noise must have awakened occupants of the adjoining apartments, felt only a small portion of the total responsibility. Realizing after a few seconds or minutes that the police should be called, each individual was able to feel that someone else must have already done it. In other words, responsibility for intervening in the emergency was so diffused to other people, that no one intervened.

This was pure speculation, and the investigators decided to meet their responsibilities as scientists by putting it to empirical test.

College students were recruited for a research project concerned with the problems of living and learning in the urban environment. They were told that they were to talk with other students about these problems, and that in order to protect personal identities, the conversation would be held over an intercom system with each student in a separate room. The experimenter himself would not listen but would get the subject's reaction later, by questionnaire. Each person was to talk for a certain length of time and then let the next person in the group speak. When everyone had spoken, they were to start with the first person again. The experimenter explained that an automatic switching device would turn the microphone on and off and that only one microphone at a time would be on.

The first person to speak was a tape-recorded confederate, hereafter referred to as the "victim." He said he found it difficult to get accustomed to New York City and his studies. Then with great hesitation, he admitted that he was prone to seizures when under pressure.

After each person in the group had spoken once, the victim opened his next contribution with a few simple comments about the difficulty of urban living. He then continued, growing increasingly louder and incoherent:

> I er um I think I I need er if if could er er somebody er er er er er er er give me a little er give me a little help here because er I er I'm er er h-h-having a a a a real problem er right now and I er if somebody could help me out it would it would er er s-s-sure be sure be good . . . because er there er er a cause I er I uh I've got a a one of the er sei - - - - - - - - - - er er things coming on and and and I could really er use some help so if somebody would er give me a little h-help ur er-er-er-er-er c-could somebody er er help er uh uh uh (choking sounds) . . . I'm gonna die er er I'm . . . gonna die er help er er seizure er (chokes, then quiet) (B. Latané and J. M. Darley, *The Unresponsive Bystander* (New York; Appleton-Century-Crofts, in press).

The dependent variable of this experiment was the amount of time between the beginning of the seizure and the instant when the subject opened the door of his cubicle. Presumably, any subject who opened his door did so in order to help or get help for the seizure victim. Whenever a subject opened his door, he was informed by an experimental assistant that the victim was now being taken care of.

Group size was the independent variable. In a *Two Person* condition, only the subject and the victim were present. Thus all the responsibility to help the victim belonged to the subject. In a *Three Person* condition, the subject and victim were joined by another student, also a tape-recorded confederate, who took his turn discussing urban living. The final condition, the *Six Person* condition, consisted of the subject, the victim, and four tape-recorded confederates. It was expected that the larger the group, the greater the diffusion of responsibility, and the slower the reaction to the victim.

This expectation was nicely confirmed. In the *Six Person* condition, only 31 per cent of the subjects opened their doors, as compared to 85 per cent of the subjects in the *Two Person* groups. Moreover, subjects in the latter condition responded faster. The *Three Person* condition produced intermediate results. It appears then that the responsibility for intervening is diffused by the knowledge that other people are also aware of the emergency.

In variations on this experiment, it was found that sex of the subject made no difference. Nor did sex of the other person in the *Three Person* groups. Various personality and background measures failed to relate to the speed of response.

Two variables have been discovered, however, which increase the likelihood that the subject will rush to the aid of the victim; these are (1) prior acquaintance with the victim, and (2) friendship with the other bystander.

Prior acquaintance with the victim was manipulated by having the subject and victim "accidentally" meet in the hall outside the experimental area just before the experiment; they chatted for two to three minutes about the introductory psychology course. There are probably two reasons that this brief encounter produced faster intervention. In the first place, subjects reported after the experiment that they could "visualize" the seizure because they had seen the person who was having it;

visualization made the seizure harder to ignore. Secondly, subjects might have been afraid that they would encounter the victim in class or in the street and be remembered as "that person who didn't help me."

Friendship with the other bystander was created simply by telling each subject to bring a close friend with him to the laboratory. The friend then took the place of the tape-recorded confederate in the *Three Person* groups. Presence of a friend completely eliminated diffusion of responsibility, and subjects responded as quickly as those in the *Two Person* groups. Darley and Latané believed this was due to the subject's need to be respected by his friend. If he did not intervene, his friend would find this out later by asking and would no longer respect him. Another possibility is that subjects did not want to make fools of themselves by over-reacting and ruining the experiment; the presence of a friend reduced their fear of responding.

The seizure experiment was a nice simulation of the murder of Kitty Genovese, but both are rather unusual emergency situations in that no one bystander knows how any of the other bystanders are responding. In the more usual case, if there is more than one bystander, the bystanders are looking at one another as well as at the victim. If it is clear to a bystander that no one else is doing anything about the emergency, there might not be a diffusion of responsibility. In order to test this possibility, Latané and Darley conducted several laboratory and field studies, all of which produced the same conclusion; we will examine only one of them here.

Male students of Columbia University were asked to come to an interview concerned with the problems of life at an urban university. Upon arriving at the laboratory, they were shown into a small room and asked to complete a pre-interview questionnaire. Subjects worked on the questionnaires alone (*Alone* condition), with two other naive subjects (*Three Person* condition), or with two experimental confederates posing as students (*Passive Confederate* condition). The latter condition is called *Passive* because the confederates were instructed to continue working on their questionnaires and to ignore the unusual event that was to occur in the room.

The unusual event was that a stream of smoke began to issue into the room from a wall vent. The chemically-produced white smoke was thick enough to obscure vision in about six minutes.

The dependent variable is obvious: when will the subject or subjects leave the room to inform someone that the building might be on fire? Darley and Latané reasoned that presence of other subjects would inhibit such an action and that the presence of two very passive confederates would inhibit it even more.

They did not believe that diffusion of responsibility would cause this because, as pointed out earlier, if it is clear that other people are not assuming the responsibility, it isn't very reasonable to talk about the responsibility being diffused. They reasoned that (1) individuals use the actions of other people to help define for themselves the meaning of an event, and that (2) when their actions are to be observed by others, they want to be very sure that the actions are appropriate to the situation.

Let us consider a subject in the *Passive* condition. He notices the smoke and looks questioningly at one or both of the confederates. The confederate looks at the smoke, shrugs his shoulders, and goes back to the questionnaire. This makes the subject feel that the smoke might not be very important (it could be a peculiarity of the heating system in this building) and it makes him feel that the confederates would consider him foolish and easily upset if he reported the smoke. Consequently, he does not leave the room to report the smoke. In fact, only 10 per cent of the subjects in this condition did so in the six minutes they were left in the room. By that time the subject had to wave the smoke away from his face in order to see the questionnaire.

Much the same thing happened in the *Three Person* condition, except that no one took the smoke quite as calmly as the confederates had in the *Passive* condition. Subjects looked at one another quizzically, talked about what it might be, and wondered what to do about it. No subject wanted to look foolish to the other subjects, and every time one looked at the others, they were still in the room—defining the situation as non-dangerous by their behavior. In only 38 per cent of these groups did one of the three group members leave the room to report the smoke.

Subjects in the *Alone* condition were also puzzled about the meaning of the smoke, but they lacked social models to suggest to them by their behavior that the smoke could be ignored. Moreover, these subjects did not have to worry about looking foolish or easily frightened. As a consequence, 75 per cent of them reported the smoke.

These and several other experiments conducted by Latané and Darley clearly show that the presence of other bystanders in an emergency situation reduces the likelihood that any one bystander will intervene. This effect is due to diffusion of responsibility and to a form of social influence in which other bystanders define the situation as not serious and simultaneously create inhibitions against acting.

15

The Risky Shift

The Risky Shift refers to a change from less risky individual decisions to more risky group decisions. Let us suppose that five Pentagon officials individually made a decision about the desirability of an eyeball-to-eyeball confrontation with a foreign power. The least risky decision would be to forego the confrontation and retain the status quo; nothing would be gained and nothing would be lost. The most risky decision would be a massive confrontation that would result either in eternal world peace or an international nuclear war. If, after making their individual decisions, the officials met in conference and made an official decision more risky than the average of their individual decisions, a risky shift would have taken place. Such changes have been shown in a wide variety of situations.

The measurement instrument ordinarily used in research on the risky shift was developed by Michael Wallach and Nathan Kogan (1964) to study individual propensities in risk-taking. In 1961, James A. F. Stoner used it to demonstrate the risky shift. Since that time, these three investigators and many others have attempted to explain the risky shift and to determine those conditions under which it would not occur. Before examining some of the experiments, let us study the measuring instrument itself.

The dilemmas-of-choice task contains twelve life-situation problems involving a central person with a choice between more or less risky courses of action. For each situation, the subject's task is to choose the lowest likelihood of success that he would accept before recommending the alternative of higher risk.

One of the risk questions is as follows:

> Mr. A., an electrical engineer, who is married and has one child, has been working for a large electronics corporation since graduating from college five years ago. He is assured of a lifetime job with a modest, though adequate salary, and liberal pension benefits upon retirement. On the other hand, it is very unlikely that his salary will increase much before he retires. While attending a convention, Mr. A is offered a job with a small, newly founded company which has a highly uncertain future. The new job would pay more to start and would offer the possibility of a share in the ownership if the company survived the competition of the larger firms.
>
> Imagine that you are advising Mr. A. Listed below are several probabilities or odds of the new company proving financially sound. Please check the lowest probability that you could consider acceptable to make it worthwhile for Mr. A to take the new job. (Kogan and Wallach, 1964, p. 256).

The alternatives available to the subject were as follows: The chances are 1, 3, 5, 7, or 9 in 10 that the company will prove financially sound.

The lowest probability of stability and therefore the riskiest decision is, of course, 1 in 10. The most conservative decision is 9 in 10. On this item and on many others, regardless of sex of subjects or group size, the decision made by a group after a period of discussion is more risky than the average individual decision made prior to discussion by the group members. It is not necessary that the discussion continue until the group has reached consensus, nor is it necessary that the post-discussion decision be made publicly. Regardless of many such variations, the risky shift occurs.

In a 1967 review of the many experiments on the risky shift Kogan and Wallach concluded the following: ". . . the phenomenon may arise from a person-centered factor of greater persuasiveness on the part of high risk-takers, from a group-

centered factor of diffusion of responsibility, or from both"
(1967, p. 262).

The best evidence for the contention that *high risk-takers
are more persuasive than low risk-takers* in group discussion is
that other group members say they are. That is, if subjects are
asked after the group discussion of the dilemmas-of-choice
situations to name the group members who had the most influence in the discussion, they name those who were most risky in
their individual judgments. Of course the choice of the high
risk-takers as persuasive might be a consequence of the risky
shift rather than a cause of it. Furthermore, the risky shift has
been found in studies in which the high risk-takers were not
selected as the most influential.

The concept of *diffusion of responsibility* suggests that an
individual making a decision alone will feel more responsibility
for failure than if he makes his decision as part of a group.
Because the riskier choices are more likely to lead to failure,
the individual will be less risky alone than in a group.

From the dilemmas-of-choice task, there is no evidence for
diffusion of responsibility. A study by Wallach, Kogan, and Bem
(1964), however, in which subjects risked money on their performance on an intellectual test, does provide some support. If a
subject felt that he was or might be solely responsible for the
wins and losses of other group members, he tended to choose
easy problems to work on; but after group discussion, he showed
a pronounced risky shift. If he did not feel responsible for the
wins and losses of other group members, there was only a small
risky shift. In other words, the greater his individual responsibility
for failure, the more pronounced the risky shift after discussion.
This result would tend to support the argument that group
discussion allowed him to diffuse his responsibility.

One of the difficulties with either the diffusion of responsibility explanation or the explanation of risk-takers being more
persuasive is that two of the twelve dilemmas-of-choice items
have frequently produced a conservative shift. And the students
of Donald Marquis have been able to write additional items
which have produced a conservative shift. Some items produce
neither a conservative nor a risky shift.

All of this led Roger Brown, in 1965, to propose that any
story-problem will to some extent engage cultural values of risk

and of caution. If it engages the risk value more strongly than the caution value, individuals making individual decisions about it will make a decision they think is risky relative to the decisions made by others. If several individuals then come together for group discussion, each will find that he is not risky, relative to the others, at all. The response to this is to become more risky, leading to the risky shift. After a while, of course, individual members stop trying to be more risky than others in the group —because while riskiness is valued, foolhardiness is not.

If the story-problem engages the value of caution more strongly than the value of risk, the individual will make what he thinks is a relatively cautious decision, will find in group discussion that it is not very cautious, and will become more cautious.

A 1968 experiment by Stoner provides some support for Brown's explanation. Using some old dilemmas-of-choice items and constructing some new ones, Stoner attempted to develop six items that would produce a risky shift and six that would produce a conservative shift.

Realizing that any dilemmas-of-choice item pits an alternative representing one value against an alternative representing a different value, Stoner abstracted from each dilemmas-of-choice item the two values; subjects were then asked to rank all the values (in all of the items) in order of their importance to them.

On the items that Stoner thought would be risk items, the alternative associated with risk did obtain a higher ranking than the one associated with conservatism, and vice versa. Thus, his intuitive feeling about the difference between items producing risky and conservative shifts proved correct at this level.

Subjects were then asked to give individual judgments about the degree of risk they would accept for each item, and the degree of risk they thought would be accepted by 200 other people like themselves.

According to the Brown hypothesis, subjects should have seen themselves as more risky than other people on the "risky" items and as more conservative on the "conservative" items.

In fact, subjects did see themselves as more risky on all six of the risky items, but as more conservative on only three of the conservative items.

Subjects then engaged in a group discussion of each dilemma. From this the shift toward riskiness or conservatism could be calculated. On all of the six risky items, there was a strong risky shift. Strangely, there was a clear conservative shift on only two of the six conservative items. These two items were among the three on which subjects had perceived themselves to be more conservative than other people. The results thus tend to support the Brown hypothesis, but they are not completely convincing.

The two items which produced a conservative shift were similar in the values they engaged: one engaged the value of "your own life," and the other the value of "the physical safety of your husband/wife." Specifically, the items producing a conservative shift were: (1) A man about to embark on a vacation trip experiences severe abdominal pains and must choose between disrupting his vacation plans in order to see a doctor or boarding an airplane for an overseas flight, and (2) A couple must choose between allowing a complicated pregnancy to continue, with danger to the mother's life, or having the pregnancy terminated.

One other item among the twelve involved the value of "the physical safety of your husband/wife," but it involved it in such a way as to lead to risk rather than to conservatism. The item was: "A person involved in an airplane accident must choose between rescuing only his child or attempting to rescue both his spouse and child with the realization that both will be lost if the attempt is unsuccessful" (Stoner, 1968, p. 447). Subjects rated the physical safety of one's spouse as more important than that of one's child, saw themselves as more risky than other people, and moved to an even riskier position after group discussion.

In other words, the value involving the physical safety of one's spouse led to a conservative shift when the conservative course of action would protect the spouse, but led to a risky shift when the risky course of action was required to save the spouse.

We conclude from this that, given an appropriate value, items can be constructed that will lead to either greater conservatism or greater risk after group discussion.

However, as shown by Stoner's inability to get conservative shifts on four of six items specifically constructed to produce such shifts, the risky shift is far easier to produce in our culture. Why this should be so and whether other cultures differ are unanswered questions.

One can think of this type of influence in terms of social comparison processes. Just as an individual practices his tennis game because there is a cultural value placed on being slightly better than other people, he changes his risk level in the direction valued by the culture so that he can feel he is slightly "better" than his peers. This does not mean that the individual automatically changes his risk level but that he reinterprets elements in the situation and focuses on arguments favoring risk.

A recent experiment by Moscovici and Zavalloni (1969) shows that the risky shift is not limited to situations involving risk, but that opinions and judgments may frequently become more polarized as a result of group discussion.

Subjects were secondary school students in Paris. They completed scales measuring their attitudes toward De Gaulle and toward the Americans, and then engaged in discussion to consensus on each item in the scales. The attitude toward De Gaulle, which was originally favorable, became more favorable as a result of group discussion. The attitude toward the Americans, which was originally unfavorable, became even more unfavorable as a result of the discussion. In short, group discussion produced a polarization of attitudes, just as group discussion has been shown to polarize acceptable levels of risk.

The results were explained on the basis of normative commitment. Group discussion makes norms or values more salient, which in turn makes arguments in support of these values more salient and convincing.

Moscovici and Zavalloni suggest that group discussion will produce an *averaging* of individual opinions when the object of judgment is not very significant to the members and there are no normative values about the object. If the object of judgment is significant and related to cultural values, group discussion will produce *polarization* of attitude.

Influence and Life

We will examine three basic questions in this final chapter: (1) In a practical sense, what are the ways to influence someone to behave as you wish? (2) In what ways are we influenced by others? (3) How should we value being susceptible to influence vs. being independent?

How can we get others to behave as we wish?

As I am writing this chapter I am living in a summer "group house" on Long Island. In my house there are, in addition to myself, four clinical psychologists, a social worker, a novelist, and an experimental psychologist named Arne. Four of the group members are chicks who insist that we eat off clean plates and that everyone share in the dishwashing. The problem is that Arne, although he is a lovely and considerate person, simply will not wash dishes.

We can use this situation to illustrate the various ways to change behavior, although to date Arne is still not washing dishes.

There are four basic ways to influence deliberately someone's behavior: request, persuade, demand, and model. First, we could simply *request* Arne to wash the dishes after dinner at least once a week. If he did not comply with the request, we could attempt to *persuade* him that he ought to.

Certain things would make it more likely that he would either comply with the request or allow himself to be persuaded. The greater his attraction to the group, the more likely it is that he would comply with the request in order to please us and protect himself against rejection. Thus we could increase his attraction to the group by, for example, being extremely nice to him. This might not work, because we would be reinforcing a behavior—not washing dishes—that we wanted to change. A better strategy would be to say "If you wash the dishes, we will introduce you to pretty girls." This is the direct use of contingent reward. We could also use punishment; "If you do not wash the dishes we will burn your bongo drums." Use of reward and punishment might work, but this is a crude and uninteresting type of influence.

If we could get Arne to comply with a small request, such as clearing his plate from the table after dinner, we might be able to employ the "foot-in-the-door" technique (Freedman and Fraser, 1966). According to these authors, complying with even a very small request produces commitment. In this case we would be hoping to produce commitment to the process of cleaning after meals. If Arne cleared his plate from the table, we could try to further increase his commitment with a slightly larger request, such as drying the wine glasses. Eventually we would make the supreme request.

We could also try to make Arne feel guilty, because it has been shown that guilt increases compliance (Freedman, Wellington, and Bless, 1967). Doing something for someone else expiates feelings of guilt. Perhaps we could fix a badminton racket so that it would break when Arne used it. Then we could immediately ask him to do us a favor of washing the dishes. There is one additional consideration in using this technique. While the Freedman et al. experiment showed that guilt increases the tendency to comply, it also found that the guilty party has a strong need to avoid contact with the person he has harmed. Thus, if we used this technique, we would need to assure Arne that Henry, the owner of the badminton set, would not be in the kitchen during dishwashing time.

Group decision might also be effective in our persuasion attempt. If all the house members got together and each publicly
committed himself to do the dishes once a week, and if we could
get Arne to make such a commitment as part of the group, he
would experience considerable pressure to keep his commitment.

If our requests and persuasion attempts all failed, we could
demand that Arne wash the dishes. We would say "The House
requires that you wash the dishes!" Hopefully, Arne would begin
to think in counter-anthropomorphic terms, seeing the House as
an impersonal entity above and beyond the house members,
a force not to be denied. If so, he would wash the dishes, not
seeing that he had any alternative.

The final technique would be to *model* dishwashing (or to
set an example). Merely washing the dishes in front of Arne
would not be effective; we would have to make dishwashing
appear to be a positive experience. The dishwashing model
could laugh, joke, dance about, pinch the chicks, and so forth.
Others in the house could thank the model and speak of him in
glowing phrases. Ultimately, Arne might think of dishwashing
as a privilege rather than a chore.

In what ways are we influenced by others?

We are often influenced because we assume, in an
ambiguous situation, that others have information that we do not
have. Greenwich Village is filled with panhandlers, people who
accost others on the street and ask for a dime for the subway,
or who simply ask if you have any spare change. (A recent article
in the *New York Times* reported that it is possible to make $200
to $300 a week doing this in some sections of the city.) A tourist
to the Village probably does not know at first whether one
should give money, refuse but try to talk, or simply ignore the
panhandler. In short, he does not know what is appropriate
behavior. If he sees someone who confidently walks by the panhandler without even acknowledging his existence, he may well
assume that the person knows the appropriate behavior and may
adopt that behavior as his own.

In general, the more ambiguous the situation, the more
likely it is that we will attribute to others greater knowledge than

we ourselves have. And the more confident they appear to be in their interpretation of the situation, the more likely it is that we will accept their behavior as information.

The example of dealing with the panhandler leads us back to a distinction made in the discussion of the Asch effect—the distinction between public compliance and private acceptance. An individual might ignore the panhandler in order to appear experienced and "cool" to any Villager who might be watching; he might feel, however, that he would like to give money if no one were watching. In other words, he has publicly complied with the example of the Villager without privately accepting that example. If the tourist were absolutely objective, he would have to believe the following: "I should have helped that poor creature, but I didn't."

This belief can be broken into two elements or cognitions: (1) I should have helped him, (2) I did not help him. According to Festinger (1957) these elements are in a *dissonant* relation to one another. Dissonance theory states that two cognitions " . . . are in dissonant relation if, considering these two alone, the obverse of one element would follow from the other" (p. 13). That is, when two elements of knowledge are inconsistent with one another, dissonance exists. Dissonance is a negative drive state which, like sexual deprivation, pain, and thirst, and so forth, motivates the individual to do something about the tension. In the example given, the tourist can either go back and give money to the panhandler or convince himself that he should not have given money.

It would be difficult for the tourist to go back and find the panhandler, to embarrass himself by changing his mind, and to appear uncool to those watching. It would not be so difficult to do some cognitive work and convince himself that the panhandler did not deserve to be helped. This is, after all, the land of opportunity; you can't help a panhandler on every corner; the guy would just use it for lush or dope anyway; and if people would quit helping the beggars, unemployment would disappear and the Great Society would appear.

In short, the tourist would reduce his dissonance by changing his attitude toward the panhandler so that it was consonant with his behavior. When examining the Asch effect, we discovered that people may publicly comply without privately accepting. We now see that public compliance leads, under some circumstances, to private acceptance.

A clever experiment by Festinger and Merrill Carlsmith (1959) illustrates one of the variables involved in this process.

Subjects who took part in the experiment were put to work for an hour on a very dull task of stacking wooden spools and turning wooden pegs. Afterwards they were induced to agree to meet the next subject to take part in the experiment and to tell him that the experiment was really very interesting. Half of the subjects were told that they would be paid $1.00 for doing this; the other half, $20.00.

The subjects who were paid $20.00 should have experienced little dissonance; they had told a small lie but had been well compensated for it. The subjects who were paid only $1.00, however, would have to justify having lied for so little money. After having accepted the money and having told the lie, the only way to reduce dissonance would be to reduce the magnitude of the lie. This could be done by privately believing that the experiment was really interesting and important.

After the lie had been told, the experimenters arranged the situation so that the subject was interviewed by another person about his reactions to the experiment. It was hypothesized that subjects paid $1.00 would like the experiment more than subjects paid $20.00, and precisely this result was obtained.

An experiment like this, and there have been several, is called a "forced-compliance" experiment. If a person can be forced to publicly comply, dissonance theory predicts that he will have a tendency to privately accept. The word "force," however, is very unfortunate. If a person is forced to do something, he can justify his behavior easily—"I had no choice." It is necessary to give the illusion of choice (which any con man or social psychologist can easily do) in order to create the conditions under which the individual must justify his behavior to himself.

When we were examining the ways to get Arne to wash dishes, we were concerned with public compliance. We did not care whether Arne enjoyed washing dishes or believed in it, we cared only that he do it. If we were concerned with creating a lasting change in attitude toward washing dishes, we would exert as little pressure as possible so that he would have to justify his dishwashing behavior with positive dishwashing attitudes. If we offered him $100.00 an evening for washing dishes we would get public compliance, but he would not wash dishes except when paid for it. If we could con him into doing it for a dime, he would have to justify his behavior by finding other compelling reasons for washing. Then he would do it privately and without financial compensation.

How should we value being susceptible to influence vs. being independent?

Our culture seems to have placed a value on being independent of social influence. We remember Thoreau as the man who marched to a different drummer. John Kennedy's *Profiles in Courage* was essentially concerned with resisting social pressure. Riesman's *The Lonely Crowd* lamented a tendency toward becoming other-directed. The lyrics of the New Music are constantly telling us to "do your own thing." The hippies are rebelling against societal pressures to conform to the college-marriage-kids-money syndrome. Young executives conform to the IBM code of dress and behavior during the day but wear false beards at night.

And yet a truly independent person, absolutely free of social influence, would be inconceivable. That man is a social animal is an inescapable fact. Our very feeling of personal identity rests on the behavior of other people toward us. We know ourselves through comparison with others, we trust our teachers to teach us, we trust our critics to recommend plays and restaurants, and we trust our friends to be honest about their perceptions of the world. We are influenced by all of these things and more, and if we were not, we would obtain little wisdom or happiness in the short time available.

About as often as you hear people say that we have become a nation of conformers, you hear them say that habits rule us too much. This is an interesting parallel. Having habits and being socially influenced are similar in that both save time—an increasingly precious commodity. If whenever you brushed your teeth you had to consider which hand to use, whether to use toothpaste or salt, whether to brush at the bathroom sink or the kitchen sink, whether it would be better to do it at another time, whether to put a towel around your neck (etc., etc., etc.), brushing your teeth would become one of the big jobs of life. Habit saves us from that. Being socially influenced saves us in much the same way.

Social influence can be a bad thing, however, and in these last paragraphs I will try to inoculate you against the two most pernicious effects of influence—hate and apathy.

Having a scapegoat makes any group more cohesive. Just as a child develops a sense of personal identify as he learns that his body is not part of the things and people around him, a group has identity to the extent that there are individuals who are clearly *not* part of the group. By directing hatred toward other individuals or groups, a group can develop a strong sense of "we-ness." We must stick together or they will destroy us. Because man desires, perhaps requires, the security of belonging to a cohesive group, this tendency to create out-groups is very strong.

The out-group may be one individual rejected by a small clique, one race hated by another, or half of the world feared by the other half. In each case the members of the group constantly reinforce one another in their hatred of the out-group. It takes great courage to resist the group pressure because there is the constant threat of rejection, the sentiment of the group being "if you are not with us, you are against us."

Apathy as a product of social influence was nicely demonstrated in the research by Latané and Darley. They demonstrated that there is a diffusion of responsibility to take action and that the presence of inactive others inhibits action.

The negative results of this diffusion and inhibition should be obvious. It results in our not helping others who clearly need help, in refusing to question or re-examine established ways of doing things, and in ignoring injustices and inequities.

Hatred and apathy were the wheels on which Senator Joseph McCarthy rode to power. What happened was: (1) In the beginning, people assumed that McCarthy had information they did not have—there were Communists in high places threatening the nation. We must stick together or they will destroy us. . . . (2) No one took the responsibility for stopping him. Thus, it appeared that no one objected. (3) Individuals had to justify their inaction by believing that, although his methods were tough, the ends justified the means. (4) Eventually, people were afraid to intervene. By not acting earlier, they had placed themselves in a vulnerable position.

Interpersonal influence is inevitable. It is good, and it is bad. I hope this book has made you more aware of the different processes. Stay alert.

References

Chapter 1

ALLPORT, F. H., *Social Psychology*. Boston: Houghton Mifflin, 1924.

DASHIELL, J. F., "Experimental studies of the influence of social situations on the behavior of individual human adults," in *Handbook of Social Psychology*, ed. C. C. Murchison. Worcester, Mass.: Clark University Press, 1935.

McDOUGALL, W., *The Group Mind*. New York: G. P. Putnam's Sons, 1920.

TRIPLETT, N., "The dynamogenic factors in pacemaking and competition," *American Journal of Psychology*, 1897, *9*, 507-533.

WHITTEMORE, I. C., "Influence of competition on performance: An experimental study," *Journal of Abnormal and Social Psychology*, 1924, *19*, 236-253.

Chapter 2

SHERIF, M., *The Psychology of Social Norms*. New York: Harper & Row Publishers, 1963. First published in 1936 by Harper & Brothers.

Chapter 3

LEWIN, K., *Field Theory in Social Science*, ed. D. Cartwright. New York: Harper & Row Publishers, 1951.

LEWIN, K., R. LIPPITT, and R. K. WHITE, "Patterns of aggressive behavior in experimentally created 'social climates'," *Journal of Social Psychology*, 1939, *X*, 271-299.

Chapter 4

ASCH, S., *Social Psychology*. New York: Prentice Hall, 1952.

——, "The Doctrine of suggestion, prestige, and imitation in social psychology," *Psychological Review*, 1948, *55*, 250-276.

LORGE, I., "Prestige, suggestion, and attitudes," *Journal of Social Psychology*, 1936, *7*, 386-402.

MOORE, H. T., "The comparative influence of majority and expert opinion," *American Journal of Psychology*, 1921, *32*, 16-20.

Chapter 5

NEWCOMB, T. M., "Persistence and regression of changed attitudes: long range studies," *Journal of Social Issues*, 1963, *19*, 3-14.

————, *Personality and Social Change*. New York: Dryden Press, 1943.

Chapter 6

BAVELAS, A., L. FESTINGER, P. WOODWARD, and A. ZANDER, "The relative effectiveness of a lecture method and a method of group decision for changing food habits," National Research Council, Bulletin of the committee on food habits.

BENNETT, E., "Discussion, decision, commitment, and consensus in 'group decision'," *Human Relations*, 1955, *8*, 251-274.

LEWIN, K., "Forces behind food habits and methods of change," *Bulletin of the National Research Council*, 1943, *108*, 35-65.

RADKE, M., and D. KLISURICH, "Experiments in changing food habits," *Journal of the American Dietetic Association*, 1947, *24*, 403-409.

Chapter 7

FESTINGER, L., "Informal social communication," *Psychological Review*, 1950, *57*, 271-282.

FESTINGER, L., H. B. GERARD, B. HYMOVITCH, H. H. KELLEY, and B. RAVEN, "The influence process in the presence of extreme deviates," *Human Relations*, 1952, Vol. V, No. 4, 327-346.

SCHACHTER, S., "Deviation, rejection, and communication," *Journal of Abnormal and Social Psychology*, 1951, *46*, 190-207.

Chapter 8

ASCH, S., "Effects of group pressure upon the modification and distortion of judgment," in *Groups, Leadership, and Men*, ed. H. Guetzkow. Pittsburgh: The Carnegie Press, 1951.

————, *Social Psychology*. New York: Prentice-Hall, 1952.

Chapter 9

FESTINGER, L., "A theory of social comparison processes," *Human Relations*, Vol. II, No. 2, May 1954, 117-140.

HOFFMAN, P., L. FESTINGER, and D. H. LAWRENCE, "Tendencies toward comparability in competitive bargaining," *Human Relations,* 1954, *7,* 2, 141-159.

Chapter 10

DARLEY, J. M., and E. ARONSON, "Self-evaluation vs. direct anxiety reduction as determinants of the fear-affiliation relationship," *Journal of Experimental Social Psychology,* Supplement 1, 1966, 66-79.

HAKMILLER, K. L., "Threat as a determinant of downward comparison," *Journal of Experimental Social Psychology,* Supplement 1, 1966, 32-39.

RADLOFF, R., "Opinion evaluation and affiliation," *Journal of Abnormal and Social Psychology,* 1961, *62,* 578-585.

SARNOFF, I., and P. G. ZIMBARDO, "Anxiety, fear, and social affiliation," *Journal of Abnormal and Social Psychology,* 1961, *62,* 356-363.

SCHACHTER, S., *The Psychology of Affiliation.* Stanford, Calif.: Stanford University Press, 1959.

SINGER, J. E., and V. L. SHOCKLEY, "Ability and affiliation," *Journal of Personality and Social Psychology,* 1965, *1,* 95-100.

WHEELER, L., K. G. SHAVER, R. A. JONES, G. R. GOETHALS, J. COOPER, J. E. ROBINSON, C. L. GRUDER, and K. W. BUTZINE, "Factors determining choice of a comparison other," *Journal of Experimental Social Psychology,* April 1969, *5,* 2, 219-232.

WRIGHTSMAN, L., "Effects of waiting with others on changes in level of felt anxiety," *Journal of Abnormal and Social Psychology,* 1960, *61,* 216-222.

Chapter 11

HENCHY, T., and D. C. GLASS, "Evaluation apprehension and the social facilitation of dominant and subordinate responses," *Journal of Personality and Social Psychology,* 1968, *10,* 4, 446-454.

ZAJONC, R. B., "Social facilitation," *Science,* 1965, *149,* 269-274.

Chapter 12

KERCKHOFF, A., and K. BACK, *The June Bug: A Study of Hysterical Contagion.* New York: Appleton-Century-Crofts, 1968.

REDL, F., "The phenomenon of contagion and 'shock effect' in group therapy," in *Searchlight on Delinquency,* ed. K. R. Eissler, New York: International Universities Press, 1949.

WHEELER, L., "Toward a theory of behavioral contagion," *Psychological Review,* 1966, *73,* 2, 179-192.

WHEELER, L., and S. SMITH, "Censure of the model in the contagion of aggression," *Journal of Personality and Social Psychology,* 1967, *6,* 1, 93-98.

Chapter 13

MILGRAM, S., "Behavioral study of obedience," *Journal of Abnormal and Social Psychology,* 1963, *67,* 4, 371-378.

————, "Liberating effects of group pressure," *Journal of Personality and Social Psychology,* 1965, *1,* 2, 127-134.

————, "Some conditions of obedience and disobedience to authority," *Human Relations,* 1965, *18,* 1, 57-76.

————, "The compulsion to do evil," *Patterns of Prejudice,* 1967, *1,* 6, 3-7.

Chapter 14

LATANE, B., and J. M. DARLEY, *The Unresponsive Bystander.* New York: Appleton-Century-Crofts, in press.

Chapter 15

BROWN, R., *Social Psychology.* New York: Free Press, 1965.

KOGAN, N., and M. A. WALLACH, "Risk taking as a function of the situation, the person, and the group," in *New Directions in Psychology, III,* ed. G. Mandler. New York: Holt, Rinehart & Winston, 1967.

————, *Risk Taking—A Study in Cognition and Personality.* New York: Holt, Rinehart & Winston, 1964.

MOSCOVICI, S., and M. ZAVALLONI, "The group as a polarizer of attitudes," *Journal of Personality and Social Psychology,* 1969, *12,* 2, 125-135.

STONER, J. A. F., "A Comparison of Individual and Group Decisions Involving Risk." Unpublished master's thesis, Massachusetts Institute of Technology, School of Industrial Management, 1961.

————, "Risky and cautious shifts in group decision: The influence of widely held values," *Journal of Experimental Social Psychology,* 1968, *4,* 442-459.

WALLACH, M. A., N. KOGAN, and D. J. BEM, "Diffusion of responsibility and level of risk taking in groups," *Journal of Abnormal and Social Psychology,* 1964, *68,* 263-274.

Chapter 16

FESTINGER, L., *A Theory of Cognitive Dissonance*. Evanston, Ill.: Row Peterson and Co., 1957.

FESTINGER, L., and J. M. CARLSMITH, "Cognitive consequences of forced compliance," *Journal of Abnormal and Social Psychology*, 1959, *58*, 203-210.

FREEDMAN, J. L., and S. C. FRASER, "Compliance without pressure: The foot-in-the-door technique," *Journal of Personality and Social Psychology*, 1966, *4*, 195-202.

FREEDMAN, J. L., S. A. WELLINGTON, and E. BLESS, "Compliance without pressure: The effect of guilt," *Journal of Personality and Social Psychology*, 1967, *7*, 2, 117-124.